MAKING
BASIC
WORK FOR YOU

MAKING *BASIC* WORK FOR YOU

Claude J. DeRossi

Systems Analyst

General Electric Company

RESTON PUBLISHING COMPANY, INC.

Reston, Virginia

A Prentice-Hall Company

Library of Congress Cataloging in Publication Data

De Rossi, Claude J.
  Making BASIC Work For You

  Includes index.
  1. Basic (computer program language) I. Title.
QA76.73.B3D47 1980 001.6'424 78-27516
ISBN 0-8359-3977-4

Also published under the title "Learning BASIC Fast".

© 1979 by
Reston Publishing Company, Inc.
A Prentice-Hall Company
Reston, Virginia 22090

10 9 8 7 6 5

Printed in the United States of America

To Dan, Lorrie, Mickey

CONTENTS

PREFACE

This text on the BASIC programming language is intended for persons who must learn the language fast. It assumes the reader knows nothing about the subject and therefore it proceeds from very fundamental concepts through to a fairly sophisticated level.

The book is written in an informal, nontechnical style. As the text builds from previous knowledge, it gives the student the ability to practice what he knows. Many examples and exercises reinforce the knowledge that the student has gained.

This book may be used in a one-semester course on BASIC programming or it may be used as a self-teaching text by the person who must learn BASIC on his own.

I would like to express my appreciation to the persons who have assisted me in this effort. In particular, I would like to thank my wife, Cindy, for her expert typing.

Claude J. DeRossi

CHAPTER 1

INTRODUCTION

The BASIC programming language was developed in the early sixties to enable persons who are not computer programmers to enlist the assistance of a computer in obtaining solutions to mathematical and business problems.

The language was developed under the direction of John G. Kemeny at Dartmouth College. Since its beginnings at Dartmouth, the language has gained greatly in popularity and is now used throughout the country on many different makes of computers.

To use BASIC, a person dials a distant computer, situated from 10 feet to 5,000 miles from where the phone is located. Then, when the computer responds with a high-pitched tone, the user places the receiver in a special cradle attached to a typewriter-like terminal. The terminal comes to life and types a message to the user. That message looks like this:

```
TIMESHARING SERVICE 4/9/78  14:28
ID—
```

The computer has identified itself and has asked the user to do the same. If the user has made previous arrangements with the computer center, he may type in a valid ID, for example:

ID—HP638

The computer checks the ID and, if it is valid, types:

SYSTEM—

The user may respond with ALGOL, FORTRAN, BASIC, PL/I, or any other programming language. The easiest of these languages to learn and to use is BASIC. The user responds:

SYSTEM—BASIC

The computer asks a question:

OLD OR NEW—

The user replies:

OLD OR NEW—NEW SIGMA

The user has indicated that he would like to give the computer a new set of instructions, the *program*, for it to execute. He names the program SIGMA. The user had the option of typing OLD if he wanted to run a program that he had previously developed and saved at the computer site. Later, we'll see how a user may call for an old saved program.

The computer types:

READY

The user is now free to type several commands constituting a program for the computer to execute. The following is a sample program that the user may enter:

```
10   DATA 5, 8, 31, 4, 16, 32, 999
20   LET S = 0
30   LET N = 0
40   READ X
50   IF X = 999 THEN 90
```

2

```
60   LET S = S + X
70   LET N = N + 1
80   GO TO 40
90   PRINT S/N
100  END
```

The user types these lines one at a time. At the end of each line, he depresses a key labeled CARRIAGE RETURN. Whenever he depresses the CARRIAGE RETURN key, the computer accepts the command that the user has just typed.

You may not understand the program shown above but don't be concerned. A sample is given here of a complete program so that you may see what a BASIC program is like. Later, we will cover in detail the meaning of the various commands used. To satisfy the curious, we might say that the program computes the average of the values, 5, 8, 31, 4, 16, and 32. Then it prints that average.

Observe the integer numbers at the beginning of each BASIC instruction. These numbers are called *line numbers*. Every instruction in BASIC must have a line number. That number may be anything the user selects so long as each line number is larger than the previous one. The line numbers of the ten instructions shown could have been 1, 18, 35, 72, 146, 208, 231, 232, 306, and 543.

Each BASIC command is called a *statement*. The sample program has ten statements. Note that there are 10 lines in the program. Each line contains a single statement.

Having completed the program, the user may now want the computer to execute it. To *execute* a program means to run it in order to obtain results. The user types:

RUN

Observe that the command RUN does not require a line number. So one must not be used.

The computer will run the program and give the answer. The answer is 16 so the computer types:

16

The user types:

BYE

3

and the "timesharing" session is over.

To recap, here is the complete conversation between computer and user:

```
TIMESHARING SERVICE 4/9/78 14:28
ID—HP638
SYSTEM—BASIC
OLD OR NEW—NEW
READY
10    DATA 5, 8, 31, 4, 16, 32, 999
20    LET S = 0
30    LET N = 0
40    READ X
50    IF X = 999 THEN 90
60    LET S = S + X
70    LET N = N + 1
80    GO TO 40
90    PRINT S/N
100 END
      RUN
      16
      BYE
                        OFF  4/9/74  14:70
```

What Have You Learned?

In this chapter, you have learned that you may call a distant computer by phone and have a conversation with it. All you need is a phone, a terminal, and a user ID.

You type your program giving statement after statement until your program has been completely entered. Having typed in a line containing a statement, you depress the CARRIAGE RETURN key. This action causes the computer to accept the last statement typed. Each statement must be preceded by a line number. Line numbers are arbitrary, but must be given in increasing sequence.

Some of the English words that are used in the BASIC programming language are:

DATA
LET

4

```
        READ
        IF
        PRINT
       *GO TO
        END
```

There are only a few more.

The two commands RUN and BYE are special words. They are not part of the BASIC language and, because of this, do not show preceding line numbers. We will discuss RUN, BYE, and several other words when we discuss *system commands* in Chapter 10.

---

*GO TO is assumed to be one word and may be written GOTO.

CHAPTER 2

USING THE SYSTEM EFFECTIVELY

There are a few facts that you must know concerning the proper way to use your terminal while programming in BASIC. We know you're anxious to begin learning the language and discovering how to use it in solving problems, but please bear with us for just one more chapter.

When you dial the computer's phone number, you will hear a high-pitched tone coming from the receiver. The tone lets you know that you are connected. Place the receiver in the special cradle attached to your terminal. You are now using a device called an "acoustic coupler."

Not all terminals are alike. You may find that there is another way to connect using your particular terminal. If so, simply ask someone around you who has used the terminal. That person will be glad to show you how to establish a connection with the distant computer.

While you are connected, you will be operating in a mode called *conversational timesharing*. The mode is called "conversational" because you and the computer interact. You type something, and the computer responds. Then you type something else, and the computer replies. In this manner, you and the computer can communicate with each other coneeming what you want to do and how you are doing.

6

For example, if you make errors, the computer will tell you about them and give you a chance to correct them.

The mode is called "timesharing" because you share the distant computer's time with many other users, hundreds of users sometimes. Since a computer is very fast and since, during much of the time that he is connected, any one user isn't asking the computer to do very much, the computer has little trouble in obeying the commands of its many timesharing users.

When the system requests an ID number, you must give a valid ID. It is easy to arrange for an ID. Be prepared to be billed once a month for the service. Monthly charges are based upon how long you are actually connected to the distant computer (approximately $5.00 per hour), the actual computer time used (approximately $1.00 per second), and the cost of leasing a terminal (approximately $150.00 per month). There are also a variety of small charges that users may avoid if they wish.

Having been supplied with a valid user ID, the distant computer asks which language you wish to use. Other languages besides BASIC are available, but BASIC is easier than all the others to learn and to use.

The system requests OLD OR NEW. If you have written a program in the past and wish to use it again, you may call for the old program provided you saved it under some file name—for example, AREACU or INTRTN. We'll show you how to save programs later. If you wish to build a new program from scratch, you reply NEW and give the new program's name.

When the system types READY, it indicates that

1. you may begin building a new program; or
2. you may begin using an old program that the system has retrieved for you.

In entering a new program, the person types a series of statements, each statement headed by a line number. If the person types the statements in haphazard sequence, the computer will put them in order according to line numbers (in increasing sequence) when the user types RUN. Before actually obeying the RUN command, the computer will check the corresponding program for errors. If the

7

user enters two statements with the same line number, the system will accept the *last* statement typed.

Later in this text, we will discuss special commands called *system commands*. You've already been introduced to two system commands, RUN and BYE. Additional system commands to be discussed soon are OLD, NEW, LIST, SAVE, and others.

None of us is perfect. When we make mistakes, we'd like to correct them in the easiest way. Here are five ways to make corrections:

1. Suppose you enter a BASIC statement and immediately find it to be incorrect. You may correct the statement by retyping it. Observe how the statement at line 10 is corrected.

       5   LET X = 25.6
       10 LET P = 6.9.8
       10 LET P = 69.8
       20 LET R = 3.94

   The second statement at line 10 replaces the first one.
   You may correct a statement whenever you discover it was typed in error. Observe how the statement at line 10 is corrected:

       10 PRINT "THIS IS A DUMO"
       20 PRINT 92 + 65
       30 PRINT 86 / 67
       40 PRINT 6 * 27
       99 END
       10 PRINT "THIS IS A DEMO"

   The second statement of line 10 replaces the first one.

2. While you are typing a line, you may discover that you've mistyped one or more characters. You may change those characters before returning the carriage. To do so, "backspace" the carriage by employing the ← symbol. The system backspaces one character position for every ←. Observe how corrections have been made in statements 10, 20, and 30 below:

       10 LET W = 7.65 ← 4
       20 LET X = 4.92 ← 37
       30 LET Z = 7.63 ←←←← 8.63

   The computer will accept the three statements as

       10 LET W = 7.64
       20 LET X = 4.937
       30 LET Z = 8.63

   Note that in some BASIC systems, the character used to backspace the carriage is not ←, but @ or \.

3. While typing a statement, you may find that you would prefer that you had not begun to type it at all. In that case, depress the CTRL and X keys simultaneously. The system will respond DEL and the statement you had begun to type will be ignored. Study how line 100 is corrected below:

```
100   LET F = 6.9
200   LET G = F + 3.6
300   LET S = G + F
200   LET F = 7 DEL
100   LET F = 7.9
```

The user had intended to correct line 100, but he began correcting line 200 instead. When the user discovered his mistake (after having typed 200 LET F = 7), he depressed the CRTL and X keys simultaneously. The system typed DEL. Thus, line 200 was not altered by the user's action.

4. To delete a statement already entered, type only its line number and then return the carriage.

Example:

```
10   LET P = 6
20   LET P = 8
30   LET Q = 7
40   PRINT P * Q
50   END
20
```

Line 20 is deleted from the program.

5. To insert a statement, select an unused line number between existing line numbers.

```
10   LET W = 4
20   PRINT W + X
15   LET X = 2
30   END
```

Line 15 is inserted between lines 10 and 20.

Now, we will actually begin a study of the BASIC programming language.

CHAPTER 3

THE *LET* STATEMENT

In learning how to use the BASIC programming language, you only need to learn a few types of statements. These types begin with the words LET, IF, PRINT, READ, GO TO, FOR, NEXT, STOP, and END; and there are only a few more.

The various statement types are identified by the first word of the statement. Thus, we may refer to a LET statement, an IF statement, a print statement, etc.

In the next few chapters, we will learn only a few statement types: the LET, IF, PRINT, GO TO, and END statements. You will see that with a knowledge of only five statement types, you are able to instruct a computer to solve an amazingly large variety of practical problems.

Let's consider the LET statement first. The LET statement is used to assign a given number or the result of a calculation to a name. Here are some examples:

11

```
10  LET P = 3.4
20  LET S = 9.1
30  LET T = 3.1 + 5.8
40  LET V = P + 5
50  LET W = P – S
```

At line 10, the value 3.4 is assigned to a computer memory cell called P. The name P holds the value 3.4. When P appears again in later statements (for example at lines 40 and 50), the value of P in those statements is that which was assigned earlier. In the example, the value used at lines 40 and 50 is 3.4.

The value 9.1 is then assigned to S. (See line 20.)

At line 30, the sum of 3.1 and 5.8 (8.9) is assigned to T.

At line 40, the sum of P (3.4) and 5 is assigned to V. That sum is 8.4. At line 50, the value of S (9.1) is subtracted from P (3.4), and the result is assigned to W. That result is –5.7.

After the five LET statements have been executed by the computer, the values of P, S, T, V and W, as they are stored in five memory cells, are these:

3.4	9.1	8.9	8.4	–5.7
P	S	T	V	W

In BASIC, the names of memory cells may consist of single letters of the alphabet such as A, B, C, P, Q, R, X, Y, Z, or a single letter of the alphabet followed by a single digit.

Examples:

A1, A2, B6, C0, E6, F9, G5

These BASIC names for memory cells are correct:

D
A8
F
H6
M
N0

These are not:

5M	(Names may not begin with a digit.)
XD	(Names may not consist of two letters.)
P6X	(Names may not contain more than two characters.)

LET statements may use the same name on both sides of the equal sign. A statement such as

50 LET D = D + 6

is correct. The *old* value of D is added to 6, and the sum of the calculation is assigned back to the memory cell called D. Therefore, if D looked like this

8.94

D

before the statement was executed; it would look like this

14.94

D

after the statement was executed.

Take note of this point: In any LET statement calling for a calculation, the entire calculation is made before the final assignment of the result to a memory cell is made.

Example:

60 LET F = G + 13.44 + F

If we assume that G's value was 9.2 and F's was 2.2 before the calculation, the entire calculation is made *before* the final assignment 60 was executed, F and G looked like this:

2.2   9.2

F   G

After the statement was executed, F and G looked like this:

| 24.84 | | 9.2 |
| F | | G |

Study the following program segment:

```
10  LET M = 6
20  LET N6 = 17.3
30  LET P = M + N6
40  LET M = M + 10
50  LET W4 = N6 − M
```

Fill in these cells with the proper values, assuming that the statements have been executed:

☐ ☐ ☐ ☐
M N6 P W4

The correct value to place in M is 16. The value originally assigned to M was 6, but later 10 was added to it. (See the statements at lines 10 and 40.)

The correct value to place in N6 is 17.3. That value was assigned at line 20. It never changed thereafter.

The correct value to place in P is 23.3. That value was assigned at line 30. At that time, M's value was 6. When M's value was changed to 16 at line 40, the computer did not back up to change the value of P that it had assigned at line 30.

The correct value to place in W4 is 1.3. The value for W4 was assigned at line 50. At that time, N6's value was 17.3, and M's value was 16.

In BASIC, names that have never been given values are assumed to contain zeroes. Thus, the program

```
10   LET A = 4
20   LET C = A + B
30   PRINT A,B,C
40   END
```

will run, but the program has been poorly written. The program will print 4, 0, and 4.

CHAPTER 4

THE *IF* STATEMENT

By using the IF statement, one may direct a program to make decisions as it executes. The following are examples of IF statements:

```
      :     additional statements in the program that are not shown
      :
100   IF A = B THEN 750
110   IF D > 6 THEN 280
120   IF 8 > X THEN 940
130   IF A * B < = 15.3 THEN 2040
140   IF A − D <> E THEN 3000
150   IF H < M/N THEN 305
      :     more statements not shown
```

In these statements the symbols =, >, <, >=, <=, <> mean, respectively:

=	equals	
>	greater than	
<	less than	
>=	greater than or equals	(=> is acceptable also)
<=	less than or equals	(=< is acceptable also)
<>	not equal	(>< is acceptable also)

17

Let's look at the first statement shown in the above examples:

100 IF A = B THEN 750

When the program encounters this statement, it will examine the values currently assigned to A and B. If the value assigned to A exactly equals the value assigned to B, the program will jump to line 750. If A's value does not equal B's, the program will go to the next statement in sequence. That statement is the one at line 110.

The IF statement at line 110 checks whether D is greater than 6. If it is, the program jumps to line 280; if not, the program goes to the next statement in sequence. That statement is at line 120.

Study the IF statements given in the examples. You'll observe that each IF statement has a relational symbol selected from the set =, >, <, >=, <=, <>. (The last three relational symbols are formed by typing two consecutive characters found on the keyboard of your terminal.)

Values shown on either side of the relational symbols may be memory cell names such as A, B, D, X, H; actual numeric values such as 6, 8, 15.3; or arithmetic expressions such as A*B, A − D, M/N.

When writing an arithmetic expression, you may use the symbols + to mean add; − to mean subtract; * to mean multiply; / to mean divide; and ↑ to mean exponentiate. Arithmetic expressions may be used in LET, IF, and (as we'll see later) PRINT statements.

For example, here is an arithmetic expression in a LET statement:

200 LET P = A+B−C*D+E/F−G↑3

The computer has been instructed to add A to B, subtract C times D, add E divided by F, and subtract G raised to the third power. The final result is assigned to P.

In an IF statement, an expression may look like this:

3005 IF D/F+H ↑ 5>K*L THEN 4050
3010 LET J = W+2

The computer is being instructed to check whether D divided by F

18

plus H raised to the fifth power is greater than K times L. If it is, the program is being told to jump to the statement at line 4050; if it is not correct, the program is being told to go to the next statement in sequence, the one at line 3010.

In a later chapter, we will discuss in greater detail how to write more complex arithmetic expressions. For now, the knowledge you have will enable you to do the problems and exercises given in the next few chapters.

GO TO in IF Statements

Many timesharing systems permit the words GO TO in place of THEN in IF statements. Thus, the IF statement

```
1000 IF X = Y THEN 2000
```

may also be written

```
1000 IF X = Y GO TO 2000
```

We prefer the exclusive use of THEN since it is the standard way to write the IF; not all systems recognize GO TO in that statement.

CHAPTER 5

THE *PRINT* STATEMENT

The PRINT statement is used for a variety of purposes. One of those purposes is to have the computer print the values that have previously been assigned to computer cells. Those statements take this form:

```
        :
        :      additional statements not shown
        :
  30   PRINT P, W, L
  45   PRINT D, D3
  58   PRINT M; T; V; Z
  59   PRINT E1, E3; E6
```

At line 30, the computer is being instructed to print the *last* values that were assigned to memory cells P, W, and L. The computer will print those values beginning in columns 1, 16, and 31 of the paper being used by your terminal.

Output paper is divided into five zones as follows:

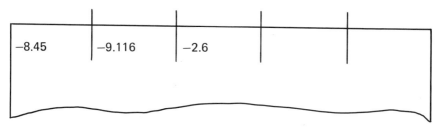

Zone 1 extends from print positions 1 through 15; Zone 2, from 16 through 30; Zone 3, from 31 through 45; Zone 4, from 46 through 60; and Zone 5, from 61 through 75. (On some terminals, print positions extend only through 72. The fifth zone is therefore shorter than the others.)

The print positions mentioned above are not actually printed on the output paper. You have to imagine their existence.

In the example above, suppose the values last assigned to P, W, and L were −8.45, −9.116, and −2.6, respectively. In response to PRINT P, W, L, the computer will print:

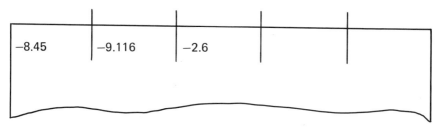

The three minus signs are located in colums 1, 16, and 31. If the three values had been positive, the three print positions would have contained blanks.

The second PRINT statement reads 45 PRINT D, D3. If the values last assigned to D and D3 were 1.848 and 5.92, respectively, the line printed would be:

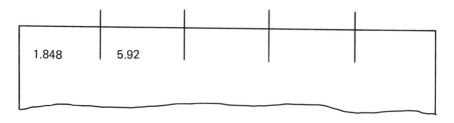

Since the two values are positive, print positions 1 and 16 are blank. The digit 1 appears in print position 2, and the digit 5 appears in print position 17.

The PRINT statement at line 58 reads:

    58 PRINT M; T; V; Z

Note that semicolons rather than commas separate the memory cell names. Semicolons cause values to be printed closer together. If the values are positive, two blanks separate one number from another; if negative, only one blank separates one number from another.

Suppose the values assigned to M, T, V, and Z are 8.2, −7.6, 9.43, and −1.5, respectively. The computer will print this line:

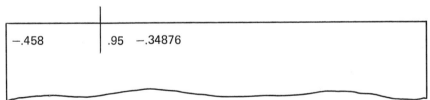

```
−8.2   −7.6      9.43   −1.5
```

Zones are ignored. The values begin in print positions 1, 6, 12, and 17, respectively.

The last PRINT statement in the example is:

    59 PRINT E1, E3; E6

If the values of E1, E3, and E6 are −.458, .95, and −.34876, respectively, the computer will print this line:

```
−.458        .95  −.34876
```

The value −.458 prints in Zone 1. The minus sign appears in print position 1. The value .95 prints in Zone 2. The decimal point in the number prints in print position 17. In the PRINT statement, a semicolon separates E3 and E6. The semicolon causes the value of E6 to print following that of E3, with only one blank separating the two values. Note the comma separating the name E1 from the name E3. The value of E1 is directed to print in Zone 1; the value of E3 is directed to print in Zone 2.

23

The PRINT statement is also used to instruct the computer to print one or more literal messages. Here are some examples:

```
500 PRINT "THIS IS A SAMPLE MESSAGE"
510 PRINT " WHICH WE ARE ASKING"
520 PRINT "   THE COMPUTER TO PRINT."
```

Observe carefully that there is no blank between the quotation marks and the letter T in the first statement; that there is one blank between the quotation marks and the letter W in the second statement; and that there are two blanks between the quotation marks and the letter T in the third statement.

When the computer prints these three lines, the character that immediately follows the quotation marks in each statement prints in print position 1 of the output paper. The computer will print these three lines.

```
THIS IS A SAMPLE MESSAGE
WHICH WE ARE ASKING
   THE COMPUTER TO PRINT.
```

Observe that the blanks that were shown in the PRINT statements have been reflected in the printed lines.

One may give the program PRINT statements that look like this:

```
650 PRINT "VALUE OF A IS";A;" OF B IS";B
```

Suppose the value of A is 91.65 and that of B is −546.8. The computer will print this line:

```
VALUE OF A IS   91.65 OF B IS −546.8
```

A careful examination of the PRINT statement shows that the V in VALUE is to appear in print position 1; that there are to be two blanks printed between the letter S in IS and the 9 of 91.65; that there is to be one blank before the letter O in the second OF; and that there is to be one blank between the letter S in the second IS and the minus sign preceding −546.8.

A third use of the PRINT statement is to have the computer print the result of a calculation made within the PRINT statement. These statements are examples:

        2500 PRINT A+B
        2510 PRINT B/2,5.3*3,A−B
        2520 PRINT A,B,B↑3,946

In response to the first PRINT statement, the computer will add A and B, then print the result. Suppose that the last value assigned to A was 10 and that the last value assigned to B was 2. The computer will print this line:

        12

The digits 1 and 2 print in positions 2 and 3, respectively.

Note that the PRINT statement may be written correctly as

        2500 PRINT A + B

but will not be correct if written as

        2500 PRINT C = A + B

The result of a calculation may not be assigned to a memory cell in a PRINT statement. Of course, the two statements

        2500 LET C = A + B
        2505 PRINT C

are perfectly admissible.

The PRINT statement

        2510 PRINT B/2,5.3*3,A−B

calls for three calculations. The computer will print:

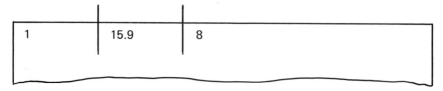

| 1 | 15.9 | 8 |

A and B still hold the values 10 and 2, respectively. The values above begin in print positions 2, 17, and 32.

The third PRINT statement

2520 PRINT A, B, B↑3,946

causes the values of A (10), B (2), B^3 (8), and 946 to print in the first four zones of the output paper. The line will look like this:

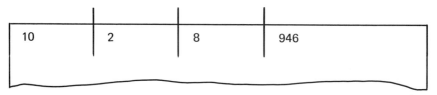

| 10 | 2 | 8 | 946 |

The four values begin in print positions 2, 17, 32, and 47.

Now consider the following illustrative program:

```
10 PRINT "THIS IS A DEMO"
20 PRINT
30 PRINT "A","B", "C"
40 PRINT
50 LET A=−6
60 LET B = 8
70 PRINT A,B,A*B
80 PRINT "END OF JOB"
90 END
```

The computer will print these lines:

THIS IS A DEMO			
A	B	C	
−6	8	−48	
END OF JOB			

The simple command PRINT, as shown in lines 20 and 40, results in a blank line.

Consider this next example:

```
350   PRINT "THIS IS A TEST"
500   PRINT 346 + 925
RUN
```

The program consists of only two statements (350 PRINT "THIS IS A TEST" and 500 PRINT 346 + 925). The command RUN tells the system to *execute* the program; that is, to give the required results. Observe that RUN is never preceded by a line number. RUN is called a *system command.* A system command is not a part of the program; it simply tells the computer what to do with programs. Some other system commands we will explore later are SAVE, LIST, OLD, NEW, BYE, and others.

After you have told the computer to run the program, the computer will examine it for typographical errors or violations of BASIC programming rules. If the computer finds none, it will run the program. When it does so, you will see these lines:

```
THIS IS A TEST
 1271
```

When building a program, you type instructions called *statements.* There are several statements that one might find in a complete BASIC program:

```
100 LET S = 0
200 FOR K = 1 to 1000
300 LET S = S + K
350 NEXT K
450 PRINT S, K
999 END
```

Don't concern yourself with what this program does, but do note these points:

1. Each statement must be preceded by a line number. Line numbers may be arbitrarily selected and may range from 1 through 99999.

27

You may select line numbers with small or large intervals between them, but they must be given in increasing sequence. If you type your statements out of sequence, the computer will automatically sort them by line number in increasing sequence.

2. Each statement must be typed and then followed by a carriage return. To type the first statement in the example, first type the line number (100), then depress the space bar, and then type the statement itself (LET S = 0). Having typed the statement, depress the CARRIAGE RETURN key. The system accepts the statement you have just typed. Other statements of the program are typed in exactly the same manner.

When you have finished typing in your program, you may ask the computer to run it for you. To do this, type the command RUN.

CHAPTER 6

THE *G O T O*
AND *E N D*
STATEMENTS

In BASIC, the IF statement is termed a *conditional transfer statement* because the computer jumps to a distant point in the program, depending upon whether or not a certain condition being tested is true or false. Thus, in

```
605 IF L < Y THEN 300
610 LET W = L + 1
```

the program jumps to line 300 if, and only if, the value of L is less than the value of Y. Otherwise, the program goes to the next statement in sequence—the one at line 610.

There is another type of transfer statement in BASIC. This is the *unconditional transfer.* It has this form:

```
810 GO TO 45
```

The program is directed to jump unconditionally to line 45. The words GO TO are always followed by a line number. The line number may be either smaller or greater than the line number at which the GO TO statement is located. Therefore, a jump may be either forward or backward in a program.

The final statement type we will consider in this chapter is the END statement. It has this form:

```
9000 END
```

There may be only one END statement in a program, and it must be located at the very end of the program. Therefore, it will have the highest line number in your program. (In some BASIC systems, the END statement is optional. It may be omitted.)

The following is an example showing how all five statement types that you've learned so far may be used in a program. Suppose we want to write a program that prints the results of

```
1 X 1
2 X 2
  :
  :
  :
  :
  :
10 X 10
```

Here is how the program could be written:

```
10  PRINT "THIS PROGRAM MAKES CALCULATIONS."
20  PRINT
30  PRINT "X","X TIMES X"
40  PRINT
50  LET X=1
60  PRINT X,X*X
70  LET X = X+1
80  IF X > 10 THEN 100
90  GO TO 60
100 END
```

At line 10, the program defines the heading that is to be printed. The "empty" PRINT statement at line 20 simply provides a blank line between the program heading and the column headings that follow.

The PRINT statement at line 30 defines the column headings. We want the character X to appear in print position 1 of the output paper and the characters X TIMES X to appear beginning at print position 16. The "empty" PRINT statement at line 40 provides a blank line between the column headings and the lines of numbers which follow.

The LET statement at line 50 assigns the value 1 to a memory cell named X.

The PRINT statement at line 60 directs the program to print the last value assigned to X and the result of the calculation X times X. Each time that the calculation is made, the last value assigned to X is the one actually used. The values of X and X times X will appear beginning in columns 2 and 17. These will always be positive values; therefore, print positions 1 and 16 will never have minus signs printed in them.

The value of X is increased by 1 at line 70. A statement such as

70 LET X = X + 1

is quite permissible in BASIC. It directs the computer to add 1 to the *old* value of X and store the result back in X. The same memory cell is used to hold the value of X. When X is updated, the old value is destroyed.

At line 80, the program checks whether the value of X is greater than 10. If so, the job has been completed and the program must stop. Otherwise, the program continues moving forward to the next statement in sequence. That statement is located at line 90.

When X is greater than 10, the program is to jump to line 100, which holds the END statement. When X is not greater than 10, the program to go to statement 90, which then gives an unconditional jump back to line 60.

At line 60, the previously executed cycle is repeated. The value of X has grown so the printed line is different from the one previously given.

When the programmer directs the computer to execute the program by typing the single word

RUN

the program will provide this output:

32

```
THIS PROGRAM MAKES CALCULATIONS

X                    X TIMES X

1                    1
2                    4
3                    9
4                    16
5                    25
6                    36
7                    49
8                    64
9                    81
10                   100
```

Now for some improvements. We can have the program center the values of X times X by changing the PRINT statement at line 60 so that it reads:

60 PRINT X, "   ";X＊X

There are three blanks between the set of quotation marks. We have directed the computer to insert three blanks in the print line beginning at print position 16. The blanks will appear in columns 16, 17, and 18. The values of X times X will print beginning in print position 20. (They would begin in 19 if they were negative; but they're not.)

You may have noticed that the program could be reduced by one statement. If the IF statement reads:

80 IF X < = 10 THEN 60

then the GO TO statement at line 90 may be eliminated. It's all right to simply delete the statement at line 90 and keep statement 100 where it is. Where line numbers are concerned, the only rule to observe is that they must be in increasing sequence. You may leave any interval you wish between line numbers.

CHAPTER 7

THE *READ* AND *DATA* STATEMENTS

The READ and DATA statements act as teammates in BASIC programs. To illustrate how these two statements work, let us study this brief program:

```
2000 DATA 17, 45, 61, 85, 92

2010 READ F

2020 PRINT 2*F, F

2030 GO TO 2010

2040 END
```

The DATA statement provides a list of values to be used in the program. Those values are accessed by one or more READ statements.

In the example, the first statement to be executed is READ F. The first value assigned to F is 17, the first value in the DATA statement. The program then doubles F and prints the doubled value and F; that is, the program prints 34 and 17. (See statement 2020.)

Next, the program returns to the READ statement. As you'll recall, GO TO is a command that directs the program to jump to a distant statement in the program. When the program executes the READ statement again, it picks up the next unused value in the DATA statement. That value is assigned to F.

The new value assigned to F is 45. That new value replaces the old value. As before, the computer prints twice F and F. Then the program returns to the READ statement again.

As you can see, the program is in a *loop*. This means that the program repeats several instructions over and over until there are no more values to be processed from the DATA statement. The program then prints a message reading

OUT OF DATA IN 2010

and stops. When the program prints the OUT OF DATA message, it tells which READ statement caused the message.

DATA statements may appear anywhere in a program so long as they precede the END statement. There may be several DATA statements in a program if more than one is required. The multiple DATA statements are considered to be the same as one continuous DATA statement.

Suppose, for example, the sample program shown at the beginning of this chapter had been this:

2000 DATA 17, 45, 61, 85, 92

2005 DATA 84, 6, 64

2010 READ F

2015 DATA 49, 58, 67

2020 PRINT 2*F, F

2022 DATA 3

2024 DATA 99, 95

2030 GO TO 2010

2040 END

The program would work exactly as it did before except that 14 data values will be processed instead of only 5. Those 14 values will be

17, 45, 61, 85, 92, 84, 6, 64, 49, 58, 67, 3, 99, 95

When the program stops, it will print:

OUT OF DATA IN 2010

You should place DATA VALUES in a program in a manner neater than that shown above. It's best to place all DATA statements either at the beginning of a program or just ahead of the END statement.

The READ statement may read more than one value at a time. Consider this program:

```
1000 READ D, E
1010 PRINT D, E, D*E
1020 READ F, G, H
1030 PRINT F, G, F*G*H
1040 GO TO 1000
1050 DATA 3, 5, 6, 4, 7, 11, 8, 33, 14, 92, 15
1060 DATA 18, 17, 2, 6
1070 END
```

The program assigns the values 3 and 5 to D and E, respectively. Then the program assigns 6, 4, and 7 to F, G, and H, respectively.

Next, the program assigns 11 and 8 to D and E, respectively; 33, 14, and 92 to F, G, and H; 15 and 18 to D and E; and 17, 2, and 6 to F, G, and H. Finally, the program prints

OUT OF DATA IN 1000

In order for a READ statement to be completely satisfied, there must be at least as many unused values still in the DATA statement as the READ statement requires. Thus, if execution of the READ statement

2090 READ W, X, Y, Z

is attempted and only three unused values still remain in the DATA statement, the program will print

OUT OF DATA IN 2090

Now let's try a practical problem. Suppose you wish to sum the values in the DATA statement shown at line 5000. Study the program which attempts to accomplish the task:

```
5000 DATA 46, 83, 94, 57, 66, 41, 13, 93, 88
5010 LET S = 0
5020 READ B
5030 LET S = S+B
5040 GO TO 5020
5050 PRINT S
5060 END
```

This program will not work. True enough, the program reads values of B and adds them to S, the sum of those values; but when the values run out, the program will stop and print the message

```
OUT OF DATA IN 5020
```

The program will not execute the statement at line 5050. It never gets there.

We need a *dummy value* located in the DATA statement; that is, a value that does not act as an actual value in the program—a dummy value that merely signals the end of the DATA. Observe below how the program has been changed.

```
5000 DATA 46, 83, 94, 57, 66, 41, 13, 93, 88, 999

5010 LET S = 0

5020 READ B

5030 IF B = 999 THEN 5060

5040 LET S = S+B

5050 GO TO 5020

5060 PRINT S

5070 END
```

The dummy value may be any value that a programmer selects, but the value ultimately chosen must not accidentally or inadvertently

38

match one of the actual values that must be processed. An IF statement is used to determine whether the dummy has been found. When the dummy is found, the program jumps to a distant statement in the program. In the example, it jumps to 5060 where the required sum is printed.

Consider a problem where the average of several values must be computed. The program will compute S, the sum of the values, and N, the number of those values. Here is the program:

```
2100 DATA 18, 48, 73, 63, 15, 35, 34, 999
2110 LET S = 0
2120 LET N = 0
2130 READ X
2140 IF X = 999 THEN 2190
2150 LET S = S+X
2160 LET N = N+1
2170 GO TO 2130
2180 PRINT S/N, S, N
2190 END
```

This program provides a little bonus. Not only does it print the average of the values, but it also prints S, the sum of the values, and N, the number of those values.

Exponential Notation

Very often, the computer gives answers in *exponential notation.* The rules that govern the time at which the computer gives answers in exponential notation vary from system to system; therefore, the user may have to obtain some experience with his system in order to predict the form the answers will take. If some of the answers are given in exponential notation, such answers usually cause no special problem if the user understands them.

Here are some examples of exponential values:

2.17346E 03   means 2.17346×10^3 or 2173.46

1.18467E 25   means 1.18467×10^{25} or

                                   11846700000000000000000000.00

When the computer gives a very large value in exponential notation, only the six non-zero digits leading the string of digits are actually precisely known by the system. Thus, if you ask the computer to calculate 11^{10}, the computer may store the answer in its memory as 2.59374E 10. This is the output the computer prints even though the actual value of 11^{10} is 25937424601.

If your programs are scientific in nature, you may also want to use exponential notation when you feed the computer numbers to work with. You may enter those numbers in DATA, LET, or INPUT statements. For example, you may write a program this way:

```
1000 DATA 2.18E5, 43, .01E4, 6.726E-4
1010 READ D
1020 LET E = (D+2.5E6)/4
1030 PRINT D,E
1040 GO TO 1010
1050 END
```

When the computer gives you answers in exponential form, it uses a rigid format:

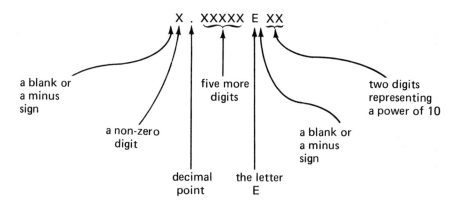

Example:

$$-3.92765E-03$$

The value of the number if -3.92765×10^{-3} or $-.00392765$.

When you write a number in exponential notation, you are permitted a good deal of flexibility. Thus, you may write the number 181389 as

```
        181389
       .181389E6
       .181389E + 06
       .181389E 06
      1.81389E5
       .0181389E7
      1813890E −1
```

and in many other ways.

A handy reference table showing powers of 10 is shown below:

EXPONENTIAL TABLE

Form		Meaning
−6	10^{-6}	(.000001)
−5	10^{-5}	(.00001)
−4	10^{-4}	(.0001)
−3	10^{-3}	(.001)
−2	10^{-2}	(.01)
−1	10^{-1}	(.1)
0	10^{0}	(1)
1	10^{1}	(10)
2	10^{2}	(100)
3	10^{3}	(1000)
4	10^{4}	(10000)
5	10^{5}	(100000)
6	10^{6}	(1000000)

The REM Statement

The REM (remark) statement is a special statement that a programmer may use in a program to give messages to himself or to some other observer. It is used to tell what is happening in a particular portion of the program. Here's an example:

```
100  DATA 3,9,4,7,8,999
110  REM DATA VALUES ARE GIVEN ABOVE
120  REM THE VALUE 999 IS A DUMMY
130  READ X
140  REM A VALUE IS ASSIGNED TO X AND
150  REM THEN CHECKED TO SEE IF IT IS THE DUMMY
160  IF X = 999 THEN 240
170  LET Y = X ↑ 3
```

41

```
180 REM THE VALUE OF X IS CUBED
190 REM AND PRINTED
200 PRINT X,Y
210 GO TO 130
220 REM THE PROGRAM RETURNS TO THE READ
230 REM STATEMENT TO OBTAIN ANOTHER VALUE
240 END
```

REM statements are printed by the computer when the user asks for a listing of his program, but they have no effect on the way the program solves the problem. The program above would have given the same result if it had been written like this:

```
100  DATA 3,9,4,7,8,999
110  READ X
120  IF X = 999 THEN 160
130  LET Y = X ↑ 3
140  PRINT X,Y
150  GO TO 110
160  END
```

It is a good idea to sprinkle REM statements liberally throughout a program. Their existence will help a person to better understand the program at some later time.

In this text, we do not use REM statements often because the accompanying paragraphs explain the programs thoroughly. We prefer to keep the sample programs as uncluttered as possible. However, in actual programming, the only explanation to be found concerning some programs may be in the REM statements that were provided. We 'do encourage you to use REMs freely in your programs.

PRINT TAB and PRINT USING Statements

The PRINT TAB and PRINT USING statements are extensions of PRINT statements. They permit greater flexibility by having the computer print information on output paper.

Let's look at PRINT TAB first. Here are some ways in which PRINT TAB may be used:

```
10  READ A,B,C,D
```

```
20  PRINT TAB (35); A;TAB(50);B;TAB(65);C
30  READ I,J
40  PRINT TAB(I);D;TAB(J);"*"
50  DATA 5.8,6.2,7.9,1.6,25,50
90  END
```

This program reads values 5.8, 6.2, 7.9, and 1.6 and assigns them to memory cells A, B, C, and D, respectively. Then it prints the values of A, B, and C beginning at print positions 35, 50, and 65. (See the PRINT statement at line 20.) The program then reads two more values, 25 and 50. It uses those values as the print positions in the PRINT statement at line 40. The value of D is printed beginning at print position 25; the asterisk (∗) is printed at print position 50. Observe that the values of A, B, C, and D are positive. Print positions 35, 50, 65, (and 25, on the next line), contain blanks.

There are 75 print positions on teletype paper numbered from 1 through 75, inclusive. (Some systems permit printing upon 72 print positions only.) If you ask the computer to print a value beginning at some given print position, the system will print the value at exactly that position if the number is negative; otherwise, the system will print the value one position to the right. Literal messages are printed beginning at exactly the print positions you designate.

When you give a program a print position, the value should be an integer. If it isn't an integer, the system truncates the non-integer portion of the value and takes the integer portion as the print position. For example, in the statement

PRINT X, Y, TAB(50.8);Z;TAB(N);"THE END"

the program will print the value of X in the first zone of the output paper; the value of Y in the second zone; the value of Z beginning at print position 50; and the message THE END beginning at print position N. If the value of N is 68.6, the system will begin the message at print position 68.

TAB values must be given in increasing sequence; otherwise, erroneous outputs will be given. For instance,

PRINT TAB(60);A;TAB(50);B;TAB(40);C

will give all the values beginning at print position 60 with one or two blanks between numbers.

43

The PRINT TAB statement may be used for plotting. Suppose we want to plot the curve $y = x^2$ from a point where x equals 1 to a point where x equals 8. A program that accomplishes the task is

```
100 LET X = 1
110 PRINT TAB(X ↑ 2);"*"
120 LET X = X+1
130 IF X < = 8 THEN 110
140 END
```

The asterisks will print at print positions 1, 4, 9, 16, 25, 36, 49, and 64 on eight lines. You may spread out the plot more by writing the program this way:

```
100 LET X = 1
110 PRINT TAB(X ↑ 2);"*"
120 LET X = X+.25
130 IF X < = 8 THEN 110
140 END
```

The PRINT USING statement may also be used for positioning values on output paper if written in this manner:

```
100 DATA 4.958, 2.71, 9.1, .053, 999

110 READ X,Y

120 IF X = 999 THEN 200

130 PRINT USING 140, X, Y

140:        #.##         #.#

150 GO TO 110

200 END
```

The program will print the values of X and Y using the information in line 140 as a guide in placing the digits. If the decimal points in line 140 are placed at print positions 13 and 24, the program will print 4.96 and 2.7 on one line of the output paper with the decimal points located at print positions 13 and 24. It will print 9.10 and .05 on the next line with the decimal points also located at print positions 13 and 24.

44

The pound signs (#) in line 140 show how many digits to give for each number on the print lines. Zeroes fill in on both sides of the decimal point if the actual values available are smaller than the pound signs given. Rounding is automatically given when applicable.

The STOP Statement

The STOP statement acts very much like an END statement, *but it may never appear at the end of a program.* The END statement is the only statement that may appear at the end of a program. A STOP statement may often be used in place of a GO TO.

Example:

```
100 DATA 9,4
200 READ A,B
210 IF A > B THEN 240
220 PRINT "A IS NOT GREATER THAN B"
230 STOP
240 PRINT "A IS GREATER THAN B"
250 END
```

The STOP statement need never be used by a programmer. The one above could have been replaced by GO TO 250.

CHAPTER 8

SOLVING PROBLEMS USING SEVEN STATEMENT TYPES

You now know how seven types of BASIC statements work. With only the READ, DATA, LET, PRINT, IF, GO TO, and END statements, you may write many programs that solve a large variety of data processing problems. Let's consider some examples.

Suppose, for example, you need a table that shows the amount of interest that one would have to pay for one year at 7½ percent simple interest on various loans ranging from $1,000 through $10,000 in steps of $1,000. The program that gives this table is this:

```
10   PRINT "TABLE OF INTEREST COSTS"
20   PRINT "      AT 7.5 PERCENT"
30   PRINT

40   PRINT "AMT OF LOAN","INTEREST COST"
50   PRINT
60   LET L = 1000

70   PRINT L, .075 * L

80   LET L = L + 1000

90   IF L < = 10000 THEN 70
```

```
100 PRINT

110 PRINT "    END OF TABLE"
120 END
```

In this program, L stands for loan amount. Observe that 7½ percent must be used in its decimal form, .075.

When you type RUN, you will receive this output:

```
TABLE OF INTEREST COSTS
    AT 7.5 PERCENT

AMT OF LOAN      INTEREST COST

1000            75
2000            150
3000            225
4000            300
5000            375
6000            450
7000            525
8000            600
9000            675
10000           750

    END OF TABLE
```

The letter A in AMT OF LOAN appears at print position 1 of the output paper; the letter I in INTEREST COST appears at print position 16. The values printed per line begin in print positions 2 and 17. The initial letter E in END OF TABLE appears at print position 4.

The actual loan and interest values can be centered more exactly under their column headings if line 70 in the program is changed to:

```
70 PRINT "  ";L, "    ";.075*L
```

There are two blanks between the first set of quotes and four blanks between the second set of quotes.

As another example, suppose you are required to compute the gross pay for five employees. The facts you need to know about these employees are shown in this table:

Employee Number	Hours Worked	Pay Rate
67046	39.5	5.50
74005	40.0	4.80
81547	38.6	5.00
83926	35.0	3.45
96149	40.0	4.25

A program to print out the gross pays is this:

```
100 PRINT "GROSS PAY REPORT"
110 PRINT
120 PRINT "EMP NUM","HRS WORKED","PAY RATE",
       "GROSS PAY"
130 PRINT
140 PRINT 67046, 39.5, 5.50, 39.5*5,50
150 PRINT 74005, 40.0, 4.80, 40.0*4.80
160 PRINT 81547, 38.6, 5.00, 38.6*5.00
170 PRINT 83926, 35.0, 3.45, 35.0*3.45
180 PRINT 96149, 40.0, 4.25, 40.0*4.25
```

The actual values given and the calculation results will be printed on each line. For example, after the headings are printed, the values printed on the next line will be 67046, 39.5, 5.50, and 217.25. These values will print beginning at print positions 2, 17, 32, and 47, respectively.

The report heading, GROSS PAY REPORT, could be better centered if you change line 100 to read:

```
100 PRINT " ","   ";"GROSS PAY REPORT"
```

There is one blank between the first set of quotes and three blanks between the second set of quotes. The program prints a blank in print position 1, then moves to the second zone of the output paper and gives three blanks ahead of the report heading. The report heading therefore begins in print position 19. (Eighteen blanks will precede the heading.)

Example:

Suppose we wish to compute and print the first 20 numbers of the Fibonacci series. The series begins this way:

0, 1, 1, 2, 3, 5, 8, . . .

Observe that each number is computed from the sum of the two preceding numbers. Thus, 3 is obtained from 1 + 2; 5 is obtained from 2 + 3; 8 is obtained from 3 + 5; etc. The following is the program that generates and prints the desired numbers:

```
10  PRINT "FIBONACCI NUMBERS"
20  PRINT
30  LET N=0
40  LET A=0
50  PRINT A
60  LET N=N+1
70  LET B=1
80  PRINT B
90  LET N=N+1
100 LET C=A+B
110 PRINT C
120 LET N=N+1
130 IF N=20 THEN 170
140 LET A=B
150 LET B=C
160 GO TO 100
170 PRINT "20 FIBONACCI NUMBERS HAVE BEEN PRINTED"
180 END
```

In this program, N counts the number of Fibonacci values that have been printed. Note that when N reaches 20, the program stops.

This program prints a zero and increases the counter N by 1. Then it prints 1 and again increases the counter N by 1. Next, it computes 0 + 1 and assigns the result to C. It prints C and again advances the counter N by 1. The value of the counter is now 3.

So that the next computation of C will be correct, the value of B (1) is moved to A and that of C (1) is moved to B. When the computer goes back to line 100, the computation of C will give the correct value, 2. C is again printed and N is again increased. The procedure described in this paragraph is repeated until the value of N reaches 20.

The statements

```
140 LET A=B
150 LET B=C
```

should be thoroughly understood. These are the statements that
assign the value of B to A and that of C to B. The order of the two
statements is also important. If the statements were interchanged,
then the value of B would be destroyed when that of C was assigned
to B. If the value of B were then assigned to A, A would receive the
value of C.

A *flowchart* of this program solution should help your understanding
of the program.* Here it is:

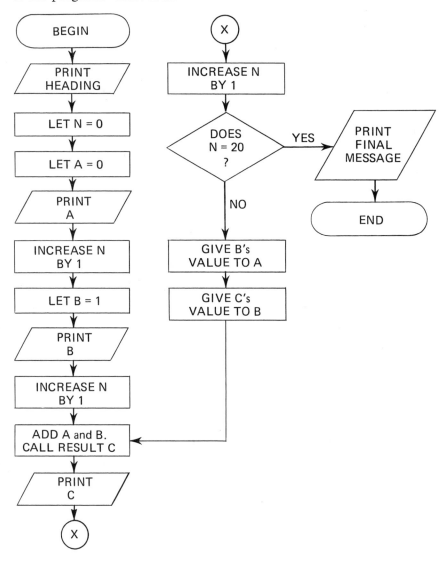

---

*Study this flowchart to get a general idea of what a flowchart is. We'll cover
flowcharting in detail in the next chapter.

Study the flowchart and follow it step-by-step with the actual numbers that the program uses. Convince yourself that when the program runs, it will give this output:

```
FIBONACCI NUMBERS

0
1
1
2
3
5
8
13
21
34
55
89
144
233
377
610
987
1597
2584
4181
20 FIBONACCI NUMBERS HAVE BEEN PRINTED
```

A Final Example

Suppose we wish to write a program that reads values from a DATA statement, sums them, and prints the average. Here is the program that accomplishes the task:

```
1000 DATA 8, 17, 15, 4, 6, 11, 4, 8, 2, 13, 999
1010 LET S=0
1020 LET C=0
1030 READ V
1040 IF V = 999 THEN 1080
1050 LET S=S+V
1060 LET C=C+1
1070 GO TO 1030
1080 PRINT S/C
1090 END
```

In the program, the values to be averaged are found in the DATA statement between the word DATA and the value 999. The value

999 is not to be summed. It simply acts as a dummy, indicating where the data ends.

The names S and C stand for *sum* and *counter,* respectively. Observe that whenever the value read, V, is not the dummy, 999, the program adds the value of V to that of S and adds 1 to the counter. Since the number of values in the DATA statement is unknown, a counter must be established to keep track of how many are read and added to S. Once the dummy value is found, the program jumps to the statement that prints S divided by C (the sum of the values divided by their number).

The statements at lines 1010 and 1020 *initialize* S and C to zero. Strictly speaking, these two statements are unneeded because BASIC normally assigns zeroes to all memory cells before a program begins. Nevertheless, initializing such statements constitutes a good programming practice since the student may at some time encounter a computer system that does not initialize memory cells to zero.

There is no need to zero initialize variables that are given other original values. For example, if the value 3.1416 must be assigned to P, give that value in one step:

```
100 LET P=3.1416
```

This assignment replaces whatever value may previously have been stored in P.

On the next page is the flowchart for the last example.

We didn't give very many details concerning flowcharts in this chapter. We'll discuss this important topic in the next chapter.

CHAPTER 9

FLOWCHARTING

When a program is simple, a programmer may dispense with drawing a *flowchart* before he writes the program. But, when a program is moderately complex or very complex, preparing a flowchart before the program is written is an almost indispensable requirement. Many programming texts ignore flowcharting—perhaps because the art of flowcharting cannot easily be taught. Nevertheless, some formal training is required, even when one is using such a simple language as BASIC.

What follows, therefore, is a brief survey of the principles behind flowcharting. We urge the student to practice flowcharting in connection with every BASIC program he writes. The techniques to be used will soon become familiar, and the student will cease to be puzzled as to how he should actually prepare flowcharts.

First, let's consider the reasons why flowcharts exist. There are two. First, by preparing a flowchart, the programmer plans what instructions he will ultimately give to the computer. He develops a diagram showing what he will tell the computer to do first, what second, etc. As he develops his flowchart, his thoughts regarding what the problem actually is and how it is to be solved crystallize.

The programmer may find himself erasing portions of his flowchart, changing others, and combining still others. At times, he may realize that his problem-solving approach was all wrong and he may decide to begin all over again.

When a programmer has finalized a flowchart, he then has a unified plan showing how he intends to instruct the computer. He may test the plan by assuming certain input values and then follow the flowchart to determine what the computer will do with those input values. He may find that the flowchart causes the program to take an unwanted path. If so, the flowchart is said to have a "bug" in it, and it will have to be changed.

Once a flowchart has been developed and debugged, the programmer may write his program with confidence that it will properly execute almost from the first attempt. (Sometimes, programs have so many bugs in them that they won't run properly until many attempts have been made.)

The second reason why flowcharts exist is to provide documentation for later use. A programmer may more easily understand what he once did or what another programmer once did if there is a good flowchart to document the program that was written. Just a few moments of extra care in the documentation of a program will often spell the difference between whether a later programmer readily understands a program or whether he will require an extensive period of time in order to do so.

Let us consider the symbols used in flowcharting. These are the main ones:

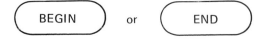

This symbol signals where a flowchart officially begins and ends. Usually, the BEGIN symbol is located in the upper left-hand corner of the first page of a flowchart. The END symbol may appear anywhere on a flowchart.

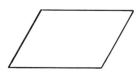

This is the *input/output symbol* and is used to indicate the reading of input data or the printing of answers.

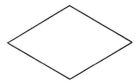

This is the *decision diamond.* A question is asked that is usually answered "yes" or "no." At least two lines must exit from a decision diamond. One is usually labeled "yes," the other, "no."

This is the *assignment symbol.* It indicates literal values to be assigned to memory cells (for example, LET D = 65); or it may indicate that a calculation and assignment is to be made (for example, LET P = Q+R).

This is the *connection symbol.* It permits the linking of one portion of a flowchart with another.

Arrows link various flowchart symbols together.

Here is one of the simplest flowcharts that one can write:

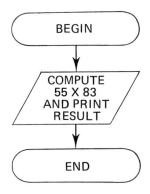

59

The BASIC program that agrees with the flowchart above is

```
100 PRINT 55*83
110 END
```

Let's try a more complicated flowchart. Suppose we want to write a program that determines which of several values in a DATA statement is the largest value. This is the DATA statement:

```
100 DATA 45, 47, 92, 18, 16, 3, 14, 999
```

The last value, 999, is a dummy and simply signals the end of the data values. Here is the flowchart with the corresponding program written beside it:

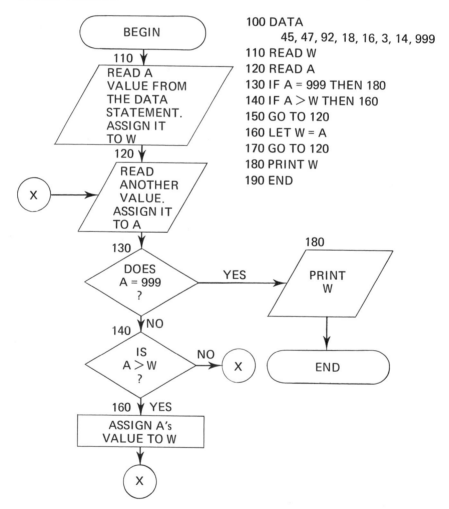

The contents of the DATA statement are never shown in a flowchart because the program is supposed to work regardless of what data are used.

Observe that a value is read from the DATA statement and is assigned to W. Now other values in the DATA statement may be checked against W. Whenever a value larger than W is read, it replaces W. When the dummy value, 999, is read, the program prints the last value which was assigned to W. This is the largest value found in the DATA statement.

If this program were saved (we'll show you how later), the program could be used many times in the future to determine the largest value of a series of values. Whenever the program is run in the future, the only statement to be changed is the DATA statement.

Observe the line numbers placed near the flowchart symbols. These numbers were placed there after the BASIC program was written. They assist one in comparing the flowchart against the corresponding program. If the program doesn't work, the reference line numbers will help the programmer determine what is wrong.

Did you notice that arrows in a flowchart show how the computer is to be instructed step-by-step. When a decision diamond is shown, the corresponding BASIC statement is the IF statement. The "no" path in a flowchart always corresponds to the statement that *follows* the IF statement.

Did you also notice that it doesn't matter what is written inside a flowchart symbol so long as the message is understandable and so long as the corresponding BASIC statement is correctly written?

Let's write one more flowchart before we leave this chapter.

Suppose we have to determine the amount of money a person will earn if he works a month (30 days) under the following conditions: he works for $.01 the first day, $.02 the second day, $.04 the third day, $.08 the fourth day, etc., until he has worked 30 days. His pay for each day is double what it was the day before.

Have the program print the amount he gets on each day and the total amount he has earned to date for each day in the month.

Here is a flowchart we can use:

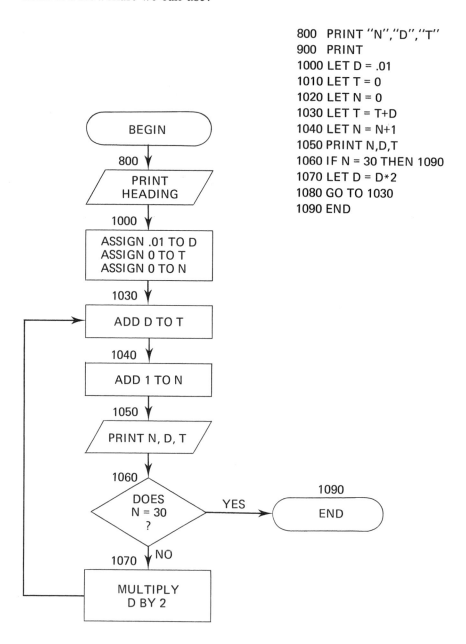

```
800  PRINT "N","D","T"
900  PRINT
1000 LET D = .01
1010 LET T = 0
1020 LET N = 0
1030 LET T = T+D
1040 LET N = N+1
1050 PRINT N,D,T
1060 IF N = 30 THEN 1090
1070 LET D = D*2
1080 GO TO 1030
1090 END
```

In this program, D holds the value that the worker has earned on any one day (.01, .02, .04, .08, etc.), T holds the total value that the person has earned to date (.01, .03, .07, .15, etc.), and N tells what day it is (1, 2, 3, 4, etc.).

The first few lines of the program's output are these:

N	D	T
1	.01	.01
2	.02	.03
3	.04	.07
4	.08	.15

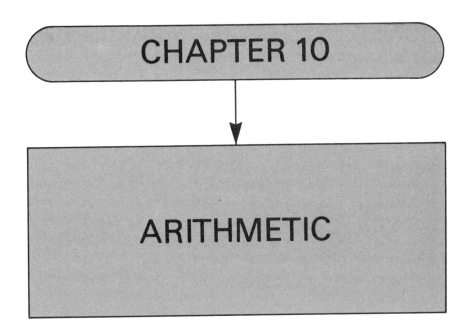

CHAPTER 10

ARITHMETIC

Computers are good at doing arithmetic. They can perform tens of thousands, sometimes millions, of calculations per second. For example, the BASIC command

105 LET F = D − E

can be performed by some computers in about one millionth of a second (one microsecond).

When you instruct a computer what calculations to make, you have to be very clear. Suppose you want the computer to give the result of this calculation:

$$\frac{41.9 + 9.5}{3.8}$$

You should not write the BASIC statement this way:

208 LET G = 41.9 + 9.5 / 3.8

The computer will think you mean

$$41.9 + \frac{9.5}{3.8}$$

65

which is quite different. The correct way to write the statement is

208 LET G = (41.9 + 9.5) / 3.8

Parentheses may be used to indicate any quantity that is to be handled as a unit.

You've seen that in BASIC the symbols that cause calculations to be made are

+ = add
− = subtract
/ = divide
* = multiply
↑ = raise to a power

In a series of calculations where parentheses are absent, the computer exponentiates first. Thus, in the statement

2400 LET D = B*C / D+E ↑ 3 − F/G

the computer will first raise E to the third power.

Second in the order of operations are multiplications and divisions. The computer scans the statement from left to right in looking for these operations. Thus, in

2400 LET D = B*C / D+E ↑ 3 − F/G

the computer will multiply B times C, then divide the result by D. Next it will divide F by G.

Last in the order of operations are additions and subtractions. In the example shown above, the result of B*C/D will be added to the result of E ↑ 3. Then, the result of F/G will be subtracted from the sum, and the final result will be assigned to D.

A table that shows the order of operations is this:

ORDER OF OPERATIONS

1. Those within parentheses
2. Exponentiations

66

3. Multiplications and Divisions
4. Additions and Subtractions

Even within parentheses, the computer uses the above chart. Thus, if there are parentheses inside of parentheses, the computer zeroes in on the innermost parentheses first. Then it looks for exponentiations, multiplications, division, etc.

A number of functions, besides the ones mentioned above, are built into BASIC to make programming easier. Some of these functions are

SIN   to obtain trigonometric sines

COS   to obtain trigonometric cosines

SQR   to obtain square roots

ABS   to obtain absolute values

LOG   to obtain natural logs

There are a few other functions that we'll discuss in Chapter 14.

Here are examples of how these functions may be used in BASIC statements:

1040 LET D = SQR (L) + SQR (2.9)

1105 LET K = LOG (P/R—S)

1150 LET T = SIN (2.1) — COS (SQR(8.1))

1160 LET V = ABS (M) + (A/B—C)

The numbers, names, or calculations shown within parentheses give the functions values with which to work. Thus, in

1040 LET D = SQR (L) + SQR (2.9)

the computer computes the square root of whatever value was last assigned to L. Then it computes the square root of 2.9. The two square roots are added and assigned to D.

In the statement

1105 LET K = LOG (P/R—S)

the computer gives the natural log of P/R−S. In computing the value of P/R−S, it uses the values last assigned to those names.

Let's write a program in which the following calculations are made:

$$F = \left[\frac{\sqrt{8.1}}{A}\right]^3 + \sin(B)$$

Assume that values of A and B are obtained from a DATA statement. Here is the program:

```
10 READ A,B
20 LET F = (SQR(8.1)/A)↑ 3+SIN(B)
30 PRINT A,B,F
40 DATA 4.5,6.6
50 END
```

At times you may wonder whether or not a set of parentheses should be included in a program. The simple rule to follow is "when in doubt, put them in." For example, this calculation

$$d = \frac{\frac{p}{d}}{f}$$

may be written as

```
1000 LET D = P/D/F
```

or

```
1000 LET D = (P/D)/F
```

But, this calculation

$$d = \frac{p}{\frac{d}{f}}$$

must be written as

```
1000 LET D = P/(D/F)
```

CHAPTER 11

SYSTEM COMMANDS

You probably recall that three commands you've used do not have line numbers. They are RUN, LIST, and BYE. These kinds of commands fall within the general category of *system commands.*

System commands are not instructions used in problem solutions. They are special messages you give the computer. RUN is a good example. This word tells the computer that you have finished typing a program and that you want it to execute that program. If the computer finds no typographical errors in your program, it will *run* it. Running a program does not mean that the answers are necessarily correct; it does mean that the computer is able to find no clerical errors and therefore can do what you have asked it to do. If you give the computer correct instructions but incorrect logic, you'll receive incorrect results.

When you enter a program by typing statements, you might make errors as you do so. Corrections can be made on the spot. Your program may tend to get a little messy, and you might want to have the computer give you an up-to-date listing of the program. The command that has the computer perform this action is LIST. Consider the following.

Example:

```
10 PRINT "PROGRAM COMPUTES SIG←NES"
20 PRINT
30 LET X = .01
30 LET X = .1
40 PRINT X, CO←←SIN (X)
50 IF X > 2 GO TO
45 LET X = X+.1
60 GO TO 40
70 END
50 IF X > 2 GO TO 70
LIST

10 PRINT "PROGRAM COMPUTES SINES"
20 PRINT
30 LET X = .1
40 PRINT X, SIN (X)
45 LET X = X+.1
50 IF X > 2 GO TO 70
60 GO TO 40
70 END
```

A close examination of the original program shows that:

1. The second line 30 replaced the first one.
2. The second line 50 replaced the first one.
3. Line 45 was placed between lines 40 and 50.
4. The corrections made in lines 10 and 40 replaced the errors.

If the programmer wants to save this program, he may type

```
SAVE
```

When the user types the word SAVE, the computer saves the program using the program name that the user gave when he began writing the program. Let's assume that in this example the user wants to save the example program under the name SINCMP.

When a user has finished working with a program and wants to have the computer begin work on a brand new program, the programmer types NEW and gives the name of the new program.

Example:

    NEW TEST

The computer responds:

    READY

Now the user may begin working on a new program. Unless he saved it, any old program he was working on that was not saved has disappeared.

Any time a user wishes to work on an old program that he once saved, he may give the message OLD and follow it with the program's name. For example, if the programmer wishes to retrieve a program called TEST, he may type

    OLD TEST

The computer retrieves TEST and types

    READY

The user may now list the program (LIST), run it (RUN), unsave it (UNSAVE), change it, or perform a number of other operations upon it.

Thus far, the words we have seen in this chapter are examples of system commands. These are

    RUN
    LIST
    OLD
    NEW
    SAVE
    UNSAVE
    BYE

As you know, when a person first signs on to the timesharing system, the computer asks him for his ID. It also requests a response to SYSTEM and a response to OLD or NEW. If the person wants to obtain an old program—one that he saved in the past—he types OLD and the name of the program under which he saved it. After the user has responded in this way, the computer retrieves his program and types

READY

From this point on, the conversation between computer and programmer proceeds as we have already discussed.

The timesharing user should be aware of the fact that when he logs onto the system, the computer makes available to him a "clean slate" in a *temporary working space.* Whatever statements he types build a program in the working space. When he gives the SAVE command, a copy is made of his working space, and that copy is stored upon his *permanent storage space.* Saving something from working space does not destroy working space. The user may continue adding to, modifying, or deleting from working space. Any time the user wants a blank copy of his working space, he types NEW again and gives a new program name. If he wants to replace an old program with the contents of working space, he types REPLACE and gives the old program name.

System commands OLD and NEW destroy the contents of a user's working space. Thus, if a programmer types

NEW BETA

or

OLD GAMMA

the "slate" in working space is destroyed. When OLD is used, the working space is given a copy of the old program named.

A word of caution: Timesharing systems vary from installation to installation. The reader may find that his system requires the words

RESAVE   instead of   REPLACE
RELEASE   instead of   UNSAVE

He may find that the symbol @ or \ must be used instead of the symbol ← in order to make character corrections in statements.

He may also find that the system may not want to know the name of his program at the time that he types NEW; it will wait for the name until the user types SAVE. If the person never saves a program, the program is never named.

If the reader remembers that systems are slightly different from installation to installation, the slight differences between them should cause no great inconvenience.

Here is a portion of a conversation that a user is having with the computer. We pick it up from the point at which the system types OLD or NEW. The person's entries are underlined.

```
OLD OR NEW—OLD INTRTN
READY
LIST
10 PRINT "THIS IS A ROUTINE WHICH"
20 PRINT "INTEGRATES THE AREA UNDER"
30 PRINT "THE CURVE OF Y=SIN(X)."
40 LET X = 2
50 LET W = .005
60 LET B = X+W/2
READY
UNSAVE
READY
OLD QUAD
READY
LIST
10 READ A,B,C
20 IF A = 5000 THEN 120
30 LET D = B ↑ 2−4*A*C
40 IF P < 0 THEN 10
50 LET U = 4*A
60 LET R1 = (−B+SQR(D))/U
70 LET R2 = (−B−SQR(D))/U
READY
50 LET U = 2*A
80 PRINT R1,R2,A,B,C
90 GO TO 10
100 END
20 IF A = 5000 THEN 100
LIST
10 READ A,B,C
20 IF A = 5000 THEN 100
30 LET D = B ↑ 2−4*A*C
40 IF P < 0 THEN 10
50 LET U = 2*A
60 LET R1 = (−B+SQR(D))/U
```

```
70 LET R2 = (−B−SQR(D))/U
80 PRINT R1,R2,A,B,C
90 GO TO 10
100 END
READY
REPLACE
READY
NEW PRIMES
PRIMES ALREADY EXISTS
NEW PRIME
READY
10 PRINT "THIS PROGRAM COMPUTES"
20 PRINT "PRIME NUMBERS"
30 LET D = 2
SAVE
READY
BYE
```

OFF AT 12:35

This user called for old program INTRTN; after listing it to see what it contained, he unsaved it.

Next, he called for QUAD, listed it, made some corrections, completed it, and resaved the program under its old name. Observe that to replace a modified program under its old name, the system command REPLACE, not SAVE, must be used. If the user had incorrectly attempted to use SAVE, the system would have typed

QUAD ALREADY EXISTS

We see an example of an error message given by the system when the user tries to create a new program called PRIMES. The system tells him he already has a program with that name. The user therefore decides to create a new program called PRIME.

After the user has entered a few lines, he sees it's time for lunch so he saves what he has done so far and signs off.

CHAPTER 12

DEBUGGING

The simplest programs you write will probably work the first time you attempt to execute them. More complex programs may not run the first time.

The computer often tells you what you have done wrong. *Error messages* are usually restricted to typographical errors. For example, if you enter

        2050 PRINT D, T, L

when you had really intended to enter

        2050 PRINT D,T,L

the computer will tell you that you have incorrect punctuation at line 2050. Or, if you give an unrecognizable command such as

        4005 MOVE A TO B

the system will tell you that there is a problem with syntax at line 4005. Usually, you will have no difficulty in determining what is wrong with a statement or the program itself when the computer gives one or more error messages.

In correcting mistakes, the programmer has to change only the incorrect statements. Sometimes he has to insert statements, or delete statements.

Let's consider some examples:

```
10 DATA 4, 17, 81, 41, 999, 0

20 REAT A,B

30 IF A = 999 THEN 200

40 LET C = A*B

50 PRIT A,B,C

60 GO TO 20

70 PRINT "END OF JOB

80 END

RUN


UNRECOGNIZABLE COMMAND IN LINE 20
UNRECOGNIZABLE COMMAND IN LINE 50
PUNCTUATION ERROR IN LINE 70
MISSING LINE 200
```

After the programmer typed RUN, the computer gave the four error messages shown. The programmer needs to correct only the statements that are wrong. Therefore, he will enter these statements:

```
20 READ A,B
50 PRINT A,B,C
200 PRINT "END OF JOB"
210 END
70
80
RUN
```

By entering 20 READ A,B, the programmer causes the new statement to replace the old one. The same applies to the statement at line 50.

By entering 200 PRINT "END OF JOB", the programmer provides

the line 200, which is required by the IF statement at line 30. He also provides a new line, line 210, to act as the new END statement. Note that this time there are two quotes in the PRINT command.

Now, lines 70 and 80 are unneeded and must be deleted from the program. To delete complete lines, the programmer types the corresponding line numbers and returns the carriage. He takes this action twice—once for line 70 and once for line 80.

When the programmer types RUN, the computer recognizes the corrections, and the program runs properly. These are the results:

4 81 END OF JOB	17 41	68 3321		

Having received his answers, the programmer may now require an up-to-date listing of his program. He types

LIST

The computer will give this response:

```
10 DATA 4, 17, 81, 41, 999, 0
20 READ A,B
30 IF A = 999 THEN 200
40 LET C = A*B
50 PRINT A,B,C
60 GO TO 20
200 PRINT "END OF JOB"
210 END
```

The programmer may now want to run the program again with new data, so he types

```
10 DATA 75, 44, 306, 94, 57, 83, 999, 0
RUN
```

The new line 10 replaces the old one. The program now gives this output:

75	44	3300		
306	94	28764		
57	83	4731		
END OF JOB				

Why is there a zero following the dummy value 999? Simply because the READ A,B statement must always read *two* values. If 999 were not followed by another value, there would not be enough numbers left in the DATA statement to satisfy the READ statement. The computer would give a message

OUT OF DATA IN 20

When a fourth attempt was made to obtain two values from the DATA statement, the program would immediately stop and the message

END OF JOB

would not print.

The computer is good at finding typographical errors, but it is not good at detecting logic errors. In the last example, if the * should have been +, the computer would not know it and could give no error message. Making sure that the answers printed out are reasonable is the responsibility of the programmer.

During the debugging of a program, the programmer may have to do some "hand" checking using a desk calculator. For example, if a program gives 1,000 answers to the command

1040 PRINT ((A*B)/(C−D)) + (E*F)

using different values of A, B, C, D, E, and F, the programmer should check a few of the results selected at random using a desk calculator. If his answers agree with those of the desk calculator, he may assume his program is debugged and accept all the answers.

Debugging techniques vary depending upon whether a job is a *one-shot job* or a *production job*. A one-shot job is a program that will be needed for only one run. It solves a problem and will never be used again. A production job is a program that will be run every day or every week, etc., with different data each time. The one-shot job will require a good deal of checking with a desk calculator before the entire set of results may be accepted. This checking will obviously be done only once.

A production job requires a good deal of desk calculator checking the first few times it is run. Since a program intended to act as a production job will probably replace a manual procedure, the computer program and the manual procedure will probably be run in parallel (parallel-checked) for a few iterations. The manual procedure will be the one actually accepted until it is abundantly clear that the computer procedure gives exactly the same results as the manual procedure. The computer program then becomes the primary method of obtaining the continuing problem solution.

In debugging a program, it may sometimes be difficult to determine exactly where the bugs lie. Suppose, for example, we have this program:

```
100 DATA 68, 45, 147, 86, 145, 26
110 READ P,Q
120 LET F = P*Q
130 LET G = F+35
140 LET H = G/2
150 PRINT P,Q,H
160 GO TO 110
170 END
```

The programmer has inadvertently told the computer to multiply P by Q when he should have told it to subtract Q from P. The answers are therefore obviously incorrect. He is getting answers in the thousands, whereas he had expected all results to be less than 100.

Looking over his program, he fails to spot the problem. (In programming, it is possible to examine the same statement over and over again and still not see an "obvious" mistake.) The programmer may resort to installing additional PRINT statements in the program so that he can follow its actions step-by-step. In the above example, the programmer might insert additional print instructions this way:

```
115 PRINT P,Q
125 PRINT F
135 PRINT G
145 PRINT H
```

Now, a listing of the program gives this:

```
100 DATA 68, 45, 147, 86, 145, 26
110 READ P,Q
115 PRINT P,Q
120 LET F = P*Q
125 PRINT F
130 LET G = F+35
135 PRINT G
140 LET H = G/2
145 PRINT H
150 PRINT P,Q,H
160 GO TO 110
170 END
```

The statements the programmer typed were inserted by the computer in the proper places in the program. Now, when the programmer types RUN, the program will print details of the calculations as they are made. The program will even verify that the READ statement worked properly too. Here is the partial output given by the program:

68	45	
3060		
3095		
1547.5		
68	45	1547.5
147	86	
12642		
12677		
6338.5		
147	86	6338.5

The programmer will now undoubtedly recognize that 3060 is a much larger value than the one he had expected for F. His attention will be drawn to line 120 of the program, where he will undoubtedly observe that LET F = P*Q should have read LET F = P–Q.

CHAPTER 13

LOOPS AND THE *FOR/NEXT* STATEMENTS

In programming, you will often want the program to repeat the execution of various statements over and over. The repetition of statements is called *looping*. The following is an example of a very simple, though costly, *loop.*

```
100 GO TO 200
200 GO TO 100
300 END
```

This is, of course, a most foolish loop. and no person in his right mind would ask the computer to perform it. Such an endless loop can be terminated in only two ways:

1. The user may hang up the phone.
2. The user may depress the BREAK or INTERRUPT key located on the keyboard.

Though some loops are inadvertent and most are useless, some types of loops are deliberately planned and are very useful.

Suppose, for example, that you have ten values in a DATA statement that must be cubed and printed. You might write this program:

```
1000 DATA 3, 19, 21, 33, 46, 74, 81, 89, 93, 105
1010 LET C = 1
```

```
1020 IF C > 10 THEN 1070
1030 READ X
1040 PRINT C,X,X ↑ 3
1050 LET C = C+1
1060 GO TO 1020
1070 END
```

The key to understanding this program is the counter, C. It has an initial value of 1. Later, that value is changed to 2, 3, 4, 5, 6, 7, 8, 9, 10, and 11. Whenever C is equal to or less than 10, the program reads a value, cubes it, then prints C, the value read, and its cube. When C is increased to 11, the statement at line 1020 detects this fact and has the program jump directly to line 1060.

Here is the flowchart that controls the execution of the above program:

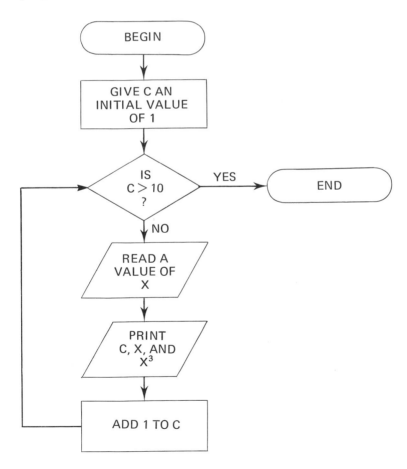

When you type RUN, the computer gives this output:

1	3	27		
2	19	6859		
3	21	9261		
4	33	35937		
5	46	97336		
6	74	405224		
7	81	531441		
8	89	704969		
9	93	804357		
10	105	1157625		

A standard flowchart skeleton that can be used whenever loops are needed is this one:

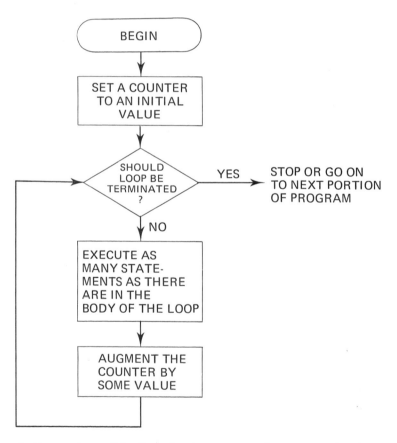

Let's see how this flowchart works against some simple problems. Suppose we wish to compute the sine and cosine of several values of

V ranging from .5 to 3.5 in steps of .1. We might use this flowchart:

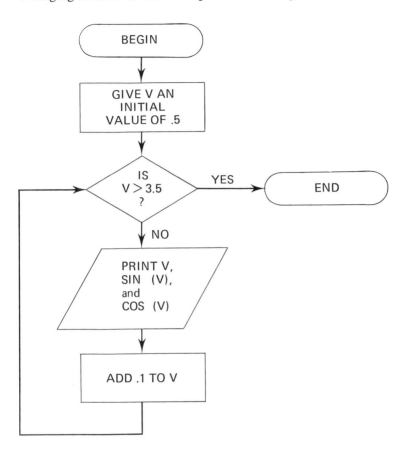

And the BASIC program:

```
500 LET V = .5
510 IF V > 3.5 THEN 550
520 PRINT V, SIN(V), COS(V)
530 LET V = V+.1
540 GO TO 510
550 END
```

Now suppose we want to compute 6 percent of all the values ranging from 10,000 through 1,000 in steps of 500. The standard flowchart (slightly modified) is used, giving this program:

```
600 LET P = 10000
700 IF P < 1000 THEN 2000
800 PRINT P, .06*P
```

```
900 LET P = P—500
1000 GO TO 700
2000 END
```

Though we have given only one statement that was to be executed in the bodies of loops in previous examples, many statements could have been given. The programmer may place as many statements in the body of a loop as he requires.

Two special BASIC statements may be used when loops are to be coded. They are FOR and NEXT. The FOR statement gives an initial value to a counter and checks for termination; the NEXT statement augments the counter. Here is an example:

```
400 FOR N = 1 TO 100
410 PRINT "THIS IS A TEST"
420 NEXT N
430 END
```

In this program, N is given an initial value of 1. N is then tested to determine whether it is greater than 100. If it is, the program jumps to the statement immediately following the line that contains the NEXT N statement. If N is not greater than 100, the program goes to the statement following the FOR statement.

At the NEXT statement, the value of N is augmented by 1, and the program is automatically directed back to the FOR statement where the loop is again tested for termination.

In this example, which simply prints THIS IS A TEST 100 times, the name of the counter is N; but it could have been any other permissible BASIC name.

Study this example:

```
300 FOR D = 10000 TO 1000 STEP —500
350 PRINT D, .06* D
360 NEXT D
370 END
```

The FOR statement shows a *step size* of −500. This means that D changes by increments of −500. The step size is a negative one, as it must be if D is to go from a high number to a lower one. In the absence of a step size, the computer always employs a step size of 1.

When a step size is positive, the termination condition is present when the value of the counter is *greater than* the given termination value. When the step size is negative, the termination condition is present when the value of the counter is *less than* the given termination value.

FOR statements may be written in a variety of ways. Here are some examples:

```
FOR Q = 10 TO 20000
FOR P6 = 3 TO 10 STEP .001
FOR F = −10 TO −4 STEP .1
FOR G = −20 TO 10 STEP 2
FOR B3 = 50 TO −50 STEP −2
FOR X = A TO B STEP C
FOR Y = P−5 TO A∗L STEP (M+N)/2
```

As you can see, the name of the counter in a FOR statement may be any desired legal BASIC name. The beginning, ending, and step-size values may be literal numbers, names, or expressions. Names must, of course, have been given values earlier in the program.

A counter in a FOR statement may act as a simple counter without acting as an actual value within the body of the loop; or the counter may act as a counter *and* an actual value. Observe that when we had the computer print THIS IS A TEST 100 times, the counter, N, did nothing but count; when we had the computer calculate interest rates for values ranging from 10,000 to 1000, the counter, D, acted like a counter *and* an actual value in the body of the loop.

Loops within loops are permissible. Consider this example:

```
1000 FOR X = 5 TO 100
1010 FOR Y = 1 TO 100
1020 PRINT X,Y, X∗Y
1030 NEXT Y
1040 NEXT X
1050 END
```

This program prints

```
5   1    5
5   2   10
5   3   15
```

etc.

The numbers on each line represent values of X, Y, and the product of X and Y. Observe that X holds the value 5 while the values of Y range from 1 through 100. Then the value of X goes to 6 and holds there while the values of Y again range from 1 to 100.

When the program ends, it will have given all possible products of X and Y with X ranging from 5 through 100 in steps of 1, and Y ranging from 1 through 100 in steps of 1. There will be 9600 products altogether.

It is important to emphasize that a counter in a loop will never exceed the maximum value given when the counter values are increasing, nor will a counter in a loop ever be less than the minimum value given when the counter values are decreasing. Thus, in a loop governed by

```
100 FOR L = 2 TO 11 STEP 3
```

the last counter value actually used in the loop is 11. The values of L will be 2, 5, 8, 11. In

```
200 FOR M = 3 TO 12 STEP 4
```

the values of M actually used will be 3, 7, 11. In

```
300 FOR P = 10 TO −3 STEP −2
```

the values of P actually used will be 10, 8, 6, 4, 2, 0, −2.

CHAPTER 14

THE *INT* AND *RND* FUNCTIONS

In earlier chapters, you saw that several BASIC functions are built-in and are available to you for the asking. These are SIN, COS, LOG, and SQR. There are a few more than a programmer may want to use. Two of them are INT and RND.

The INT function gives the largest integer value available in a given expression. For example, in

```
400 LET W = INT (25.6)
```

the value assigned to W is 25. The INT function does not round. Any fraction in the value is deleted. Here are some additional examples:

```
420 LET A = 45.8

430 LET B = 16.3

440 LET C = 8.1

450 LET D = −8.4

460 LET E = INT (B)

470 LET F = INT (C)
```

```
480 LET G = INT (A+C)

490 LET H = INT (B+D)

490 LET J = INT (A+B)

500 LET K = INT (D)
```

In this program segment, the value assigned to E is 16; that assigned to F is 8; to G, 53; to H, 7; to J, 62; and to K, −9. That last result may surprise you. Mathematicians define the largest integers of negative numbers to be the next value in the negative direction. Thus, the integer value of −8.8 is −9, and the integer value of −8.1 is also −9.

The INT function may be used to round values within certain limits. Suppose we wish to round V to the nearest integer. We add .5 to V and then take the integer of the result.

Example:

```
100 LET A = INT (V+.5)
```

If the value of V is 4.3, the value assigned to A will be 4; if the value of V is 4.7, the value assigned to A will be 5.

V can be rounded to any desired number of places. Use this relationship:

```
200 LET A = INT (V*T+.5)/T
```

where T is a power of 10; that is, T may be $10^0 = 1$; $10^1 = 10$; $10^2 = 100$, etc.

Suppose V has the value 5.634, and we wish to round it to two decimal places. The value of T will be 100 (10^2). Now

```
5.634 x 100 = 563.4
```

Adding .5, we get 563.9. The integer of this value is 563; and 563 divided by 100 gives 5.63. If V had been 5.636, the result would have been 5.64.

INT may be used to determine whether an integer is odd or even. Use this IF statement:

94

```
300 IF INT (N/2)*2 = N THEN 400
350 next statement in the program
```

If the value being tested, N, is even, the program will jump to statement 400; otherwise, it will go to the next statement in sequence.

The RND function gives a random value from 0 to 1. (The value 0 may actually be given, but the random number can never be quite as large as 1).

Consider this example:

```
110 LET D = RND (X)
```

The computer will give some number to D, a number that was not known to the programmer when he wrote the program. That number might be

```
.369485
.842314
.006394
.000000
.999999
.500000
```

or any of many other numbers. If line 110 is within a loop, the computer will give many values to D. The following, for example, is a program that gives 2000 random numbers.

```
1000 FOR F = 1 to 2000
1100 PRINT RND (X)
1200 NEXT F
1300 END
```

Any number within the range defined above has as good a chance as any other number of being printed on each line. Because each number has as good a chance as any other number, the number that actually is printed is said to be a *random number.* Thus, it appears as if the numbers that actually were given could have been drawn out of a box that contained all possible numbers. The same number could be selected two or more times in a row, but such a possibility is remote.

Observe that the RND function requires that some value be placed within parentheses. That value may simply be X as shown. If you actually have an X value in your program, there will be no conflict. It does not matter whether or not X has any other use in the program. The two actions are independent of each other. Therefore this statement is correctly written:

1500 LET E = RND (X)

whether or not X is used elsewhere in the program for some other purpose.

In the above example, you could have repeated the 2000 random values by simply typing RUN again. This feature is useful for debugging purposes, but the user might want completely unpredictable numbers. To obtain unpredictable numbers that cannot be repeated, the user must type RANDOM at the very first line of his program.

Example:

```
1000 RANDOM
1010 FOR N = 1 TO 2000
1020 PRINT RND (X)
1030 NEXT N
1040 END
```

The computer will give a set of 2,000 random values. Should the program be executed over and over, the 2,000 value sets will be different.

Random numbers are used to simulate events that take place in real life. Suppose we want to investigate what happens when a coin is tossed 10,000 times. We want to know approximately how many heads we'll get and approximately how many tails.

We'll simulate the tossings by asking the computer to give us 10,000 numbers at random. We'll agree that if any number lies betwen 0 and .5 (including 0 but not .5), the number will indicate that a head was tossed and that if the number lies between .5 and 1 (including .5 but not 1), the number will indicate that a tail was tossed.

Here's the flowchart of a program we may write:

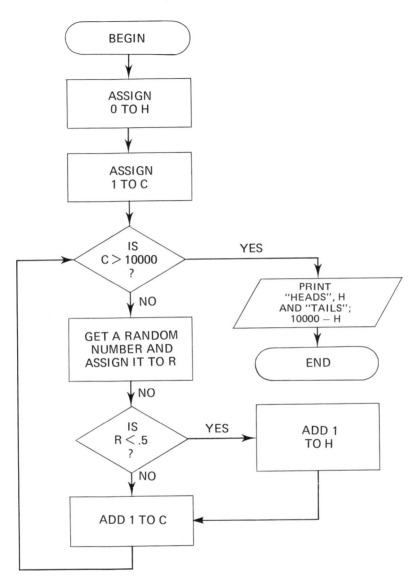

The program is

```
 90 RANDOM
100 LET H = 0
110 LET C = 1
120 IF C > 10000 THEN 300
130 LET R = RND (X)
140 IF R < .5 THEN 200
150 LET C = C+1
```

```
160 GO TO 120
200 LET H = H+1
210 GO TO 150
300 PRINT "HEADS"; H; " TAILS"; 10000-H
310 END
```

If you study the program, you'll see that H keeps track of how many heads were obtained. There is no separate count for tails since after 10,000 tosses have been made, the number of tails that were obtained may be computed by subtracting the number of heads from 10,000. In the program, H counts the number of heads obtained, and C counts the number of tosses. When C reaches 10,001 (10,000 tosses simulated), the test has been completed. (An actual run of this program gave 5,056 heads and 4,944 tails.)

Of course, only one execution of this program may give misleading results. The program should be run several times. An easy way to accomplish this objective is to insert these statements:

```
95 FOR G = 1 TO 10
305 NEXT G
```

The program will now make ten simulations and give the result for each one. An examination of the results should give a clear indication of what would happen in real life if someone were ambitious enough to toss a coin 10,000 times.

At times, the random number given by the RND function is not very useful in its raw form. It may be desirable to change it to an integer within some given range. To accomplish this, we may combine INT and RND in this way:

```
100 LET P = INT (RND(X))*15) + 6
```

The random number given by RND (X) will be converted to some integer value between 6 and 20 inclusive. The 15 indicates how many numbers are within the range, and the 6 indicates the beginning number of the range. If RND (X) gives .3, the number assigned to P will be 10; if RND (X) gives .001, the number assigned to P will be 6; finally, if RND (X) gives .999, the number assigned to P will be 20.

For reference, here is the rule:

```
1000 LET N = INT (RND(X)*R) + B
```

N is the random integer desired

R represents the number of different values possible within the range

B represents the beginning value in the range

Here's another example showing how random numbers may be useful. Suppose a TV station, operating a "dialing-for-dough" show wants to obtain ten random seven-digit telephone numbers that begin with 371. The program to obtain them is

```
10 FOR K = 1 TO 10
20 PRINT INT(RND(X)*9999)+3710001
30 NEXT K
40 END
```

The program gives telephone numbers between 371-0001 and 371-9999 inclusive. There are 9,999 numbers within the range. The beginning number in the range is 371-0001; the last is 371-9999.

CHAPTER 15

THE *INPUT* AND *RESTORE* STATEMENTS

The input data for a BASIC program is usually provided by the DATA statement. When data is read, it may be examined, accumulated, printed, or used in many other ways.

In previous examples, we have shown that the data was read only once. Data may, however, be read many times. The RESTORE command permits data to be read over and over. Here is an example:

```
100 DATA 4, 5, 7, 3, 2, 1, 3, 8, 4, 6, 7, 9
110 READ A,B,C,D
120 PRINT A,B,C,D
130 READ E,F,G
140 PRINT E,F,G
150 RESTORE
160 READ H,K
170 PRINT H,K
180 READ L,M,N,O,P
190 PRINT L,M,N,O,P
200 END
```

The first READ statement assigns 4, 5, 7, and 3 to A, B, C, and D, respectively. After printing these values, the program executes the next READ statement, which assigns 3, 2, and 1 to E, F, and G, respectively. After printing these values, the program executes the RESTORE command. A "pointer" moves back to the beginning of the DATA statement. The next READ obtains the values 4 and 5 and assigns them to H and K. The final READ statement obtains the values 7, 3, 2, 1, and 3 and assigns them to L, M, N, O, and P.

The RESTORE command therefore permits the reading of data as many times as is required.

The last program didn't do much. Let's consider a more practical example. Suppose we have these DATA statements:

```
100 DATA 14563, 94, 14605, 16, 14712, 107, 15539, 88
110 DATA 16514, 27, 16630, 3, 17021, 211, 17524, 9
120 DATA 17536, 45, 17683, 7
```

The DATA statement contains ten sets of values. Each set contains two numbers. The first number in each set represents a part number and the second number represents a quantity on hand. The numbers in each set are related. This means that there are 94 units on hand of part 14563, 16 units of part 14605, etc.

Suppose we must write a program that accepts part number inputs from the keyboard of the terminal, searches the DATA statement until the part number is found, and then prints both the part number and the quantity on hand.

A flowchart showing the problem solution is on the next page.

Here is the corresponding program:

```
100 DATA 14563, 94, 14605, 16, 14712, 107, 15539, 88
110 DATA 16514, 27, 16630, 3, 17021, 211, 17524, 9
120 DATA 17536, 45, 17683, 7
130 INPUT X
140 IF X = 0 THEN 230
150 READ Y
160 IF X = Y THEN 190
170 READ Z
180 GO TO 150
190 READ Q
200 PRINT X, Q
210 RESTORE
220 GO TO 130
230 END
```

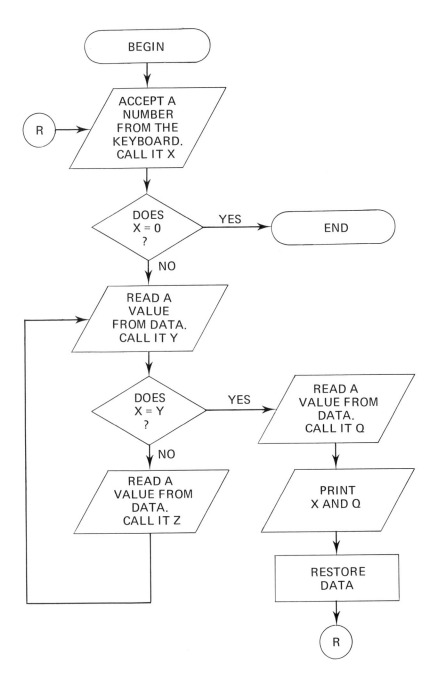

This program shows the INPUT statement in this text for the first time. When the computer executes INPUT, it types a question mark upon the terminal paper. The computer is requesting that you type a value. In the example, that value will be assigned to X. The value represents a part number.

Having accepted a value of X, the program checks to see whether you have typed zero. If you did, the execution of the program ends. If not, the program searches the DATA list until it finds the value you gave.

Having found the part number being searched for, the program reads the next number, Q. That value represents the quantity on hand of the part. Then the program prints the part number and the quantity on hand. Next, the program restores the data in the DATA statement and goes back to the INPUT statement to accept another part number to search for. The search for the new part is initiated at the beginning of the DATA statement.

In the program, when X does not equal Y, the program "throws away" the quantity on hand of Y by reading the next value, calling it Z. Z is never used.

When you type RUN, the program gives this output:

?14605				
14605	16			
?17021				
17021	211			
?0				
READY				

The program printed all the output shown above except for the part numbers following the question marks. These were typed by the user.

The INPUT statement may ask for more than one value. Suppose the INPUT statement reads like this:

500 INPUT A,B,C

When the computer prints a question mark, the user will have to type in three values separated by commas. If he types fewer than or more than three, the program will automatically print

INPUT IN WRONG FORMAT—PLEASE RETYPE

The user may then type the three numbers that are required.

As you can see, the INPUT statement permits interaction between the computer and the programmer. The computer types a message, and the user responds; then the computer types a message again, and the user responds again; the "conversation" continues for as long as is necessary to solve the problem.

Here is a segment of a math-teaching program that a programmer might create:

```
10 PRINT "HI, LET'S LEARN MATH."
20 PRINT "TELL ME, HOW MUCH IS 6 TIMES 8?"
30 INPUT A
40 IF A = 48 THEN 70
50 PRINT "NO, THAT'S NOT RIGHT.  TRY AGAIN."
60 GO TO 30
70 PRINT "VERY GOOD!"
80 PRINT "WHAT IS THE SINE OF 30 DEGREES?"
90 INPUT S
100 IF S = .5 THEN 130
110 PRINT "SORRY, THAT'S NOT RIGHT.  TRY AGAIN."
120 GO TO 90
130 PRINT "RIGHT!"
140 LET C = 1
150 PRINT "NOW, WHAT IS THE SQUARE ROOT OF 144?"
160 INPUT R
170 IF R = 12 THEN 240
180 LET C = C+1
190 IF C>3 THEN 220
200 PRINT "THAT'S NOT CORRECT.  TRY AGAIN."
210 GO TO 160
220 PRINT "PLEASE ASK YOUR INSTRUCTOR FOR HELP."
230 GO TO 2000
240 PRINT "GOOD!"
        .  additional
        .  statements not shown
        .
        .
        .
2000 END
```

The program could run for hours teaching math, science, or English. Observe that, beginning at line 140, the program gives the student three chances to answer a question concerning the square root of 144. It's a good idea to put a wrong-answer counter in a teaching program so that the learner won't give the wrong answer too many times, thus wasting expensive computer time.

.

CHAPTER 16

ARRAYS AND SUBSCRIPTS

There are times when using data directly from a DATA statement in order to solve a problem is extremely difficult if not impossible. It is true that by using RESTORE, one can have the values in a DATA statement read over and over. Nevertheless, there are times when it would be better if all the data values in a DATA statement were transferred to a working area of the computer's memory and the program then worked directly with that area.

In order to learn how to transfer values from the DATA statement and how to work with the values once the transfer has been accomplished, we must first learn how to use the DIM statement.

The DIM statement takes these forms:

    200 DIM X (50)

    210 DIM A (200), C (300), R (150)

We are directing the computer to set aside 50 memory cells all named X. In addition, we are directing the computer to set aside 200 cells called A, 300 cells called C, and 150 cells called R. (You may give several DIM statements in a program if you need them.) For convenience, we may *think* of the memory cells in the above example as if they were arranged this way:

X	A	C	R	
0	0	0	0	←First R cell
0	0	0	0	←Second R cell
0	0	0	0	←Third R cell
0	0	0	0	←Fourth R cell
				etc.

X	A	C	R	
0	0	0	0	←147th R cell
0	0	0	0	←148th R cell
0	0	0	0	←149th R cell
	0	0	0	←150th R cell
		0		

The illustration shows that when the memory cells are set aside, they are given initial values of zero.

Since all X cells look alike and have the same name, we must devise a method of distinguishing one from another. (We have the same problem with A, C, and R cells.) This is where *subscripts* enter the picture. A subscript is an integer number, or a calculation or a name representing an integer number. When placed in parentheses, the subscript number tells *which* X, A, C, or R we are interested in. Here, for example, are some statements that use subscripts:

```
100 DIM F (15)

110 LET F (3) = 4.9

120 LET F (14) = 3.34

130 LET F (15) = F(3)+8

        .
        .
        .
        .
        .
        .
        .
```

This program segment first sets aside 15 memory cells called F. Then it assigns the value 4.9 to the third F memory, the value 3.34 to the 14th, and the value 12.9 to the 15th.

After these instructions have been executed, the F values look like this:

F

0
0
4.9
0
0
0
0
0
0
0
0
0
0
3.34
12.9

The group of values shown above is called an *array*. There are 15 values in the array, and the name of the array is F. An array is established by use of a DIM statement. (See line 100 in the example.)

The DIM statement that sets up an array may be located anywhere in a BASIC program, but it must precede the program's use of the array.

The numbers shown within parentheses are examples of subscripts. Subscripts *point* to particular cells of an array. Subscripts may neither be zero nor negative numbers; they may never be larger than the maximum size of the array. In the example, subscripts may range from 1 through 15.

Arrays may contain thousands of cells. The maximum sizes permitted vary from system to system. You're almost always all right if you stay with a size of 1000 or less. It's also all right to set up a maximum array size and then actually use less cells than the maximum.

Now let's transfer some values from a DATA statement to an array:

100 DATA 3, 16, 14, 6, 8, 7, 9, 18, 21, 1, 5, 12

```
110 DIM P(12)

120 FOR K = 1 TO 12

130 READ P(K)

140 NEXT K
        .
        .
        .
```

This program segment reads 12 values from the DATA statement and assigns the values to P. Observe that the subscript used in line 130 is not an actual integer number, but rather a name representing the number. The value assigned to K will vary from 1 by 1 until the value of K actually reaches 12 and is used as a subscript with that value.

Here is what array P looks like before the FOR/NEXT loop has been executed:

P

0
0
0
0
0
0
0
0
0
0
0
0

And here is what the array looks like after the FOR/NEXT loop has been executed:

P

3
16
14
6
8
7
9
18
21
1
5
12

Having placed these 12 values in an array, we may now direct the program to work with them. Suppose the next portion of the example program does this:

.
.
.
.
.

```
150 FOR N = 1 TO 12

160 PRINT N, P(N)

170 NEXT IN
```

The program will print 12 lines. Each line will contain a number ranging from 1 through 12 inclusive and one of the 12 values of P. You'll see this output:

1	3			
2	16			
3	14			
4	6			
5	8			
:	:			
:	:			

Now suppose the 12 values must be printed in reverse order. We may add these statements:

.
.
.
.

```
180 FOR L = 1 TO 12

190 PRINT P (13—L)

200 NEXT L
```

The program computes the first subscript from the expression 13—L. Since L contains the value 1 when the FOR/NEXT loop is executed for the first time, 13—L gives the value 12. Therefore, the 12th cell location of the P array is printed. Then L changes to 2, 13—L changes to 11, and the computer prints the 11th cell location of P. The last time the FOR/NEXT loop is executed, the value assigned to L is 12. The expression 13—L gives 1, and the computer prints the first value in the P array.

The examples given above have shown that subscripts may be actual integer numbers;
Example:

        2000 LET D = P(3)

        2100 PRINT P(11)

or that subscripts may be names;
Example:

        2000 PRINT P(L)
        2300 LET F = F+P(N)

or that subscripts may be the integer results of computations.
Example:

        3000 LET M = W+P(13—J)
        3010 PRINT P(13-N)

It's important to observe that any given array does not always have to be accessed by the use of the same subscript name. In the examples above, the array P was accessed by subscripts named K, N, and L among others. Nevertheless, it is all right for a programmer to use the same subscript name. A FOR statement always reinitializes a subscript name to the beginning value shown right in the statement.

Here's a problem that in itself doesn't do much, but is educational because many programs use the technique in solving more compli-cated problems. Suppose we have this DATA statement:

        10 DATA 18,9,7,14,6,4,1,17,21,16,2,12,3,11,5

We wish to write a program that transfers these 15 values to the computer's memory. Then, the computer will examine the values one by one, interchanging values until the largest drops to the bottom of an array. Here is a program that accomplishes this task:

```
10 DATA 18,9,7,14,6,4,1,17,21,16,2,12,3,11,5

20 DIM W(15)

22 FOR J = 1 TO 15

24 READ W(J)

26 NEXT J

30 FOR K = 1 TO 14

40 IF W(K+1) > = W(K) THEN 80

50 LET T = W(K)

60 LET W(K) = W(K+1)

70 LET W(K+1) = T

80 NEXT K

90 PRINT W(15)

100 END
```

This program examines 14 pairs of numbers. (K varies from 1 through 14.) The first pair of numbers comprises the values

18 18   W(K) (the first cell of the array)

and

9 9   W(K+1) (the second cell of the array)

IF W(K+1) is larger than or equal to W(K), the numbers are in sequence and do not have to be touched. If the value of W(K+1) is not greater than or equal to W(K), then W(K) must be larger than W(K+1). The two numbers are not in sequence, and the two values must be interchanged. Three BASIC statements are needed to interchange the values. The example shows that when an interchange is needed, the value at W(K) is stored temporarily in a cell called T; the value at W(K+1) is assigned to W(K); and finally, the value stored at T is assigned to W(K+1). We can visualize the procedure by looking at this diagram:

114

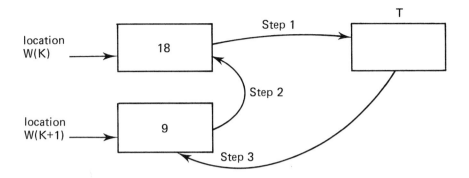

If only two statements were used to make the interchange, one of the two values would be destroyed. For example,

50 LET W(K) = W(K+1)

60 LET W(K+1) = W(K)

sets both values to the one located at W(K+1).

In the example, whenever the value of K is increased by 1, a new pair of values is examined. When the value of K reaches 14, the pair of values looked at are

W(14)

and

W(15)

The loop is terminated and the largest of the 15 numbers is definitely found at the 15th cell location of W.

In this chapter, we have merely discussed the mechanics of setting up arrays and of accessing them using subscripts. We should discuss some more practical examples than were given in the explanation. In the next chapter, we'll show how arrays may be used to sort values or to search tables.

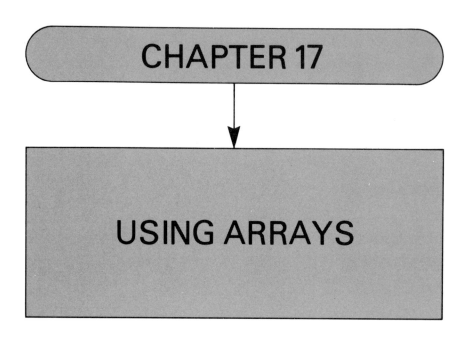

CHAPTER 17

USING ARRAYS

Problems often involve the sorting of numbers. Arrays may be effectively used as an aid in sorting a collection of numbers.

There are many techniques that may be used in sorting. The *bubble sort* is one of the easiest to understand and to use. Let's use this method to sort in increasing sequence the 12 values in this DATA statement. (Assume increasing sequence is always required.):

100 DATA 44,24,18,56,6,78,21,27,18,34,15,31

The first objective of the sort program is to place these values in an A array consisting of 12 computer cells:

A

44
24
18
56
6
78
21
27
18
34
15
31

118

Now the program is to examine 11 pairs of numbers starting at the bottom of the array. If a pair of numbers is already in ascending sequence, the program is to leave the numbers as they are; if the numbers are out of sequence, the program is to interchange the two values. In the example, the first pair of numbers examined, 15 and 31, is already in increasing sequence; therefore, the program leaves them alone.

The next pair of numbers to be examined contains the values 34 and 15. Since they are out of sequence, the program interchanges the two values:

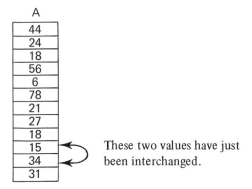

These two values have just been interchanged.

The next step is to test the next pair, 18 and 15. Since these two values are out of sequence, the program interchanges them. The array now looks like this:

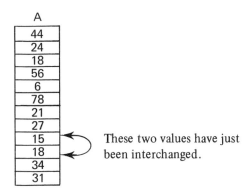

These two values have just been interchanged.

In like fashion, the program works its way toward the top of the array. Having completed this procedure, the program has placed the smallest number in the array at the top of the array. It is said that the value 6 has *bubbled up* to the top of the array. The array looks like this:

```
      A
    ┌────┐
    │  6 │
    │ 44 │
    │ 24 │
    │ 18 │
    │ 56 │
    │ 15 │
    │ 78 │
    │ 21 │
    │ 27 │
    │ 18 │
    │ 34 │
    │ 31 │
    └────┘
```

Of course, the values have not yet been sorted. A second pass is needed. The program does not bother looking at the top cell of the array since it is known without question that the top cell of the array contains the smallest value. When the second pass through the array is completed, the second smallest number is located in the second cell of the array from the top. The array looks like this:

```
      A
    ┌────┐
    │  6 │
    │ 15 │
    │ 44 │
    │ 24 │
    │ 18 │
    │ 56 │
    │ 18 │
    │ 78 │
    │ 21 │
    │ 27 │
    │ 31 │
    │ 34 │
    └────┘
```

The second pass is not the last pass. Since there are 12 numbers in the array, a maximum of 11 passes may be needed. Each pass will be shorter than the one preceding it. The last pass needs to examine only the bottom two numbers of the array. The flowchart on the following page governs how the program is to be run:

Here is the program:

```
100 DATA 44,24,18,56,6,78,21,27,18,34,15,31
100 DIM A(12)
```

120

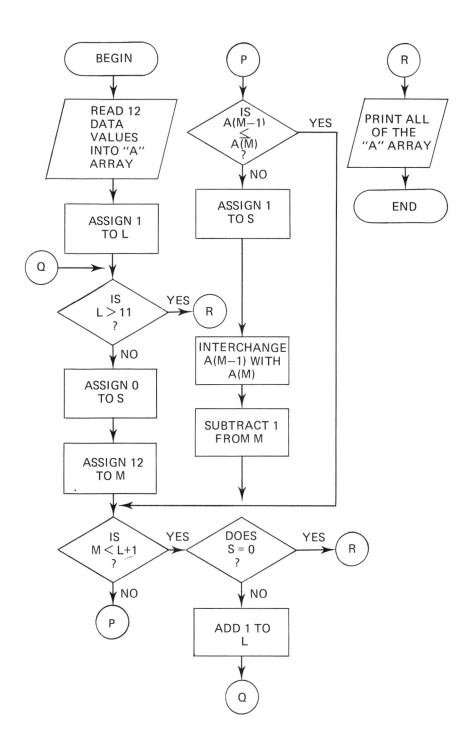

```
120 FOR K = 1 TO 12
130 READ A(K)
140 NEXT K
150 FOR L = 1 TO 11
160 LET S = 0
170 FOR M = 12 TO L+1 STEP −1
180 IF A(M+1)<=A(M) THEN 230
190 LET S=1
200 LET T = A(M−1)
210 LET A(M−1) = A(M)
220 LET A(M) = T
230 NEXT M
240 IF S = 0 THEN 260
250 NEXT L
260 FOR N = 1 TO 12
270 PRINT A(N)
280 NEXT N
290 END
```

In this program, L counts the maximum number of passes the program must make to sort the 12 numbers. That maximum is 11. The value of M governs the length of each pass. The first pass accesses A values from A(12) to A(2). See statement 170 and note that L+1 equals 2 during the first pass. Each value accessed is compared with the one immediately preceding it. See statement 210; there, the subscript M permits the examination of two consecutive values. The second pass accesses A values from A(12) to A(3). (The value of L+1 equals 3.)

The value S checks for early termination of the sort. After the completion of a pass, if the value of S is 0, the program will terminate early since no exchange of values was made during the pass. Examine line 190. You'll see that the value of S changes from a 0 to a 1 whenever even one exchange of values is made during a single pass.

The rest of the program should be self-explanatory. Observe that lines 120 through 140 read the data values to be sorted into the A array while lines 260 through 280 print out the sorted values.

In BASIC, one may set up *two-dimensional arrays.* This task is accomplished with DIM statements that look like this:

```
100 DIM B(4,5)
```

The 4 in the statement refers to the number of rows in the array and the 5 refers to the number of columns. One may visualize this array as follows:

B

0	0	0	0	0
0	0	0	0	0
0	0	0	0	0
0	0	0	0	0

Array B has
4 rows and
5 columns.

One may install values into a two-dimensional array in this way:

```
100 DIM B(4,5)

110 DATA 3,7,8,4,0,5,6,8,4,9,7

120 DATA 6,6,0,1,8,9,3,2,4

130 FOR K = 1 TO 4

140 FOR N = 1 TO 5

150 READ B (K,N)

160 NEXT N

170 NEXT K
```

We have a loop within a loop. The value of K is initialized at 1, and the values of N then vary from 1 to 5 inclusive. Subsequently, K goes to 2 and holds at 2 while values of N vary from 1 to 5 again. The procedure repeats with K going to 3 and holding, and then going to 4 and holding. The values of K and N vary step-by-step in this way:

Row (K)	Column (N)
1	1
1	2
1	3
1	4
1	5
2	1
2	2
2	3
2	4

Row (K)	Column (N)
2	5
3	1
3	2
3	3
3	4
3	5
4	1
4	2
4	3
4	4
4	5

Since K and N provide the row and column subscripts for the array B, the 20 values read from the DATA statement are stored in B this way:

B

3	7	8	4	0
5	6	8	4	9
7	6	6	0	1
8	9	3	2	4

Now, let's look at what would happen if the statement at line 150 were changed from

150 READ B(K,N)

to

150 READ B(N,K)

In the latter statement, N represents rows and K represents columns. The values of subscripts K and N are still generated as they were before. Therefore, the 20 values in the DATA statement are stored in the B array as follows:

B

3	0	4	6	9
7	5	9	0	3
8	6	7	1	2
4	8	6	8	4

Now let's try a practical application of two-dimensional array. First, set up this array:

T

246	6
255	18
261	21
275	0
283	45
294	17
298	19
306	4
315	163
326	17
335	3
343	81
356	46
364	18
375	16

The values in the left column represent part numbers; the values in the right column represent quantities on hand. We are to write a program that obtains a part number from the keyboard, finds it in the left-hand column of the T array, and prints out both part number and quantity on hand. The flowchart for this program is on the next page.

Here is the program:

```
100 DATA 246,6,255,18,261,21,275,0,283,45
110 DATA 294,17,298,19,306,4,315,163,326,17
120 DATA 335,3,343,81,356,46,364,18,375,16
130 DIM T(15,2)
140 FOR J = 1 TO 15
150 FOR K = 1 TO 2
160 READ T (J,K)
170 NEXT K
180 NEXT J
190 INPUT X
200 IF X = 0 THEN 290
210 FOR J = 1 TO 15
220 IF T(J,1) = X THEN 270
230 IF X<T(J,1) THEN 250
240 NEXT J
250 PRINT "X NOT IN TABLE",X
260 GO TO 190
270 PRINT T(J,1), T(J,2)
280 GO TO 190
290 END
```

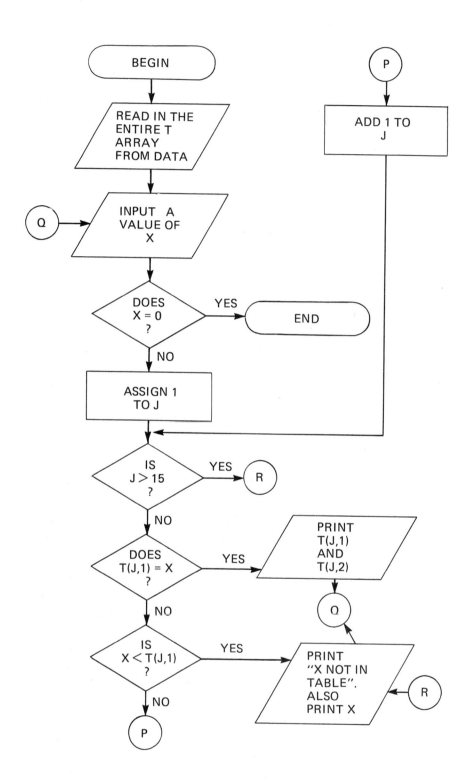

Let's observe a few points before we leave this program. First, note that the T array is a 15 by 2 array. This means that it has 15 rows and two columns. It is possible to search only the first column (the one that holds the part numbers) by holding the column subscript at 1 while varying the row subscript from 1 by 1 through 15. In the example, J is the subscript that controls the row.

At line 230, the program checks to see whether further searching in the table will be fruitless. Observe that the part numbers are arranged in numerically increasing sequence. When X, the part number we are seeking, is smaller than the part number being examined in the table, further searching of the table is hopeless and the search should be discontinued. The program prints a message notifying observers that the part number being searched for is not in the table. Then it gives the user another opportunity to enter the correct part number.

Note that the same message is printed if the search loop between lines 210 and 240 is completely performed and the value of X is not found.

The user tells the program to cease functioning by typing 0 when the program requests another X value.

Finally, study the action of the READ loops that transfer the values in the DATA statement to the T array. The outer loop, which controls the rows, varies from 1 through 15 while the inner loop, which controls the columns, varies from 1 through 2. The subscripts thus generated run as follows:

Row	Column
1	1
1	2
2	1
2	2
3	1
3	2
4	1
4	2
.	
.	
.	
.	
.	
14	1
14	2
15	1
15	2

127

Since the data values have been recorded in the DATA statement in the order in which the subscripts will accept them, the values are stored properly in the T array.

CHAPTER 18

MATRIX OPERATIONS

A *matrix* is a rectangular or square array of numbers. Typically, it is established by a DIM statement designating the name of the array and its size. A loop is generally employed to load the array with numbers.

In BASIC, several statement types are available to make working with matrices easy. As an introduction to matrix operations, let's consider the MAT READ and MAT PRINT statements. Study this example program that does not use MAT statements:

```
100 DIM Q(5,5)
110 FOR R = 1 TO 5
120 FOR C = 1 TO 5
130 READ Q(R,C)
140 NEXT C
150 NEXT R
160 FOR R = 1 TO 5
170 FOR C = 1 TO 5
180 PRINT Q(R,C)
190 NEXT C
200 NEXT R
210 DATA 3,6,7,9,15,17,18,21,24,30
220 DATA 33,40,42,43,45,47,49,51,58,63
230 DATA 65,78,84,85,87
240 END
```

The program has a loop within a loop to read values into the Q array. In the loops, R stands for row and C stands for column. (Any names besides R and C could have been selected, but these names help us understand how the array is loaded.) The array is loaded this way:

Rows ───► 1 2 3 4 5 ◄─── Columns

	1	2	3	4	5
1	3	6	7	9	15
2	17	18	21	24	30
3	33	40	42	43	45
4	47	49	51	58	63
5	65	78	84	85	87

The portion of the program that reads values into the array varies C more rapidly than R. Thus, R holds at 1 while C cycles from 1 through 5; then R advances to 2 and holds there while C cycles from 1 to 5 again. So it goes until the array is loaded.

The next portion of the program has a loop inside a loop that prints out the array. Again, R stands for row and C stands for column:

Consider the same program using matrix statements:

```
100 DIM Q(5,5)

110 MAT READ Q

120 MAT PRINT Q

130 DATA 3,6,7,9,15,17,18,21,24,30

140 DATA 33,40,42,43,45,47,49,51,58,63

150 DATA 65,78,84,85,87

160 END
```

You can see that MAT READ Q does as much work as

```
FOR R = 1 TO 5
FOR C = 1 TO 5
READ Q(R,C)
```

```
NEXT C
NEXT R
```

and MAT PRINT Q does as much work as

```
FOR R = 1 TO 5
FOR C = 1 TO 5
PRINT Q(R,C)
NEXT C
NEXT R
```

The MAT READ and MAT PRINT statements deal with values "row-rise"; that is, the first row of the array is taken care of, then the second row, then the third, etc., for as many rows as there are. Therefore, when one places values in the DATA statement and he knows they will be processed by a MAT READ statement, he must put those values in the DATA statement in sets that contain a row of values per set.

If the MAT READ and MAT PRINT statements say nothing about dimensions, the dimensions given in the DIM statement apply. Thus, in the previous example, the MAT READ and MAT PRINT statements automatically used 5 by 5 dimensions.

But a program may redefine the array being read and printed in this manner:

```
100 DATA 3,6,7,9,15,17,18,21,24,30
110 DATA 33,40,42,43,45,47,49,51,58,63
120 DATA 65,78,84,85,87
130 DIM Q(5,5)
140 MAT READ Q(3,4)
150 MAT PRINT Q
160 END
```

Despite the fact that Q is dimensioned as a 5 by 5 array, the MAT READ statement redimensions it, and Q will be read as a 3 by 4 (3 rows by 4 columns) array.

In memory, the Q arrays are loaded as follows:

Rows →	1	2	3	4 ← Columns
1	3	6	7	9
2	15	17	18	21
3	24	30	33	40

The MAT PRINT instruction *remembers* the redefinition and prints the array as follows:

| 3
15
24 | 6
17
30 | 7
18
33 | 9
21
40 | |

Don't try to write a MAT PRINT statement in this manner:

```
MAT PRINT Q(3,4)
```

It won't work. Simply write

```
MAT PRINT Q
```

If Q is redimensioned in the corresponding MAT READ statement, the MAT PRINT statement will automatically use that redefinition. Otherwise, it will use the dimension in the DIM statement.

When redefining a MAT READ statement, one may use names instead of numbers in the redefinitions—assuming that values have earlier been given to those names. Thus

```
MAT READ (X,Y)
```

is legal if values of X and Y have been assigned earlier.

Now, what about the other MAT statements?

Zero

A matrix may be set to all zeroes. Here's an example:

```
10 DIM W(6,6), X(10,10)
20 MAT W = ZER
30 MAT X = ZER (4,4)
40 MAT PRINT W,X
50 END
```

In this example, the entire W array is loaded with zeroes; only 4 rows by 4 columns of the X array are filled with zeroes. The MAT PRINT command uses the full 6 by 6 array when printing the W array and the redefined 4 by 4 array when printing the X array.

The "zero" statement may be written as

MAT Y = ZER(M,N)

if M and N have previously been assigned values.

Constant One

This MAT operation works in a manner similar to that of the "zero" statement except that the array is filled with ones. The MAT statement is written as follows:

MAT C = CON

or

MAT D = CON(6,7)

or

MAT D = CON(M,N)

An associated MAT PRINT statement remembers a dimension redefinition if such a redefinition has been made.

Identity

An identity matrix may be established by writing statements such as

MAT H = IDN

or

MAT J = IDN(5,8)

or

$$\text{MAT P = IDN(P,Q)}$$

An identity matrix is a two-dimensional array having ones along a diagonal and zeroes in all other cells.

Any dimension redefinition that might have been made is remembered by the associated MAT PRINT statement.

Only four MAT instructions may show dimension redefinitions. These are READ, ZER, CON, and IDN. The remaining matrix operations discussed in this chapter must use the dimensions given in the DIM statements.

Add

The form of this matrix statement is

$$\text{MAT E = A + B}$$

Each element of the A array is added to the corresponding element of the B array, and the sum is stored in the corresponding element of the E array. All three names—E, A, and B—must be dimensioned. These dimensions are actually the ones used.

Subtract

The form of the statement is

$$\text{MAT F = A} - \text{B}$$

Each element of the B array is subtracted from the corresponding element of the A array, and the difference is stored in the corresponding element of the F array. All three names—F, A, and B—must be dimensioned. These dimensions are the actual ones used.

Multiply

The form of this matrix operation is

MAT G = A * B

Each element of the A array is multiplied by the corresponding element of the B array, and the result is assigned to the corresponding element of the G array. All three names—G, A, and B—must be dimensioned. These are the actual dimensions used.

Only two arrays may be given on the right-hand side of the equal sign, but, of course, several multiplication operation statements may be given in sequence.

Multiply by a Constant

The form of this matrix operation is

MAT R = 3 * Y

or

MAT S = B * Y

or

MAT T = ((D+E)/F) * Y

Each element of the Y array is multiplied by the constant given in the statement (3 in the first example, B in the second example, (D+E)/F in the third example), and the result is assigned to the corresponding element of the array named on the left-hand side of the equal sign (=). All array names—R, S, T, and Y—must be dimensioned. Those dimensions are the ones used.

The next two MAT operations are especially useful to mathematicians. They are the INVERT and TRANSPOSE matrix statements.

Invert

The form of this matrix operation is

MAT U = INV(A)

The matrix A is inverted, and the result is assigned to the matrix U. The matrices U and A must be dimensioned. Those dimensions are the ones used.

After a matrix has been inverted, BASIC makes available a value called DET. This is the determinant of the matrix and may be printed.

Example:

    100 DATA 7,4,9,2,4,5,6,4,1,8,7,6,6,1,2,8

    110 DIM A(4,4), B(4,4)

    120 MAT READ A

    130 MAT B = INV(A)

    140 PRINT DET

    150 MAT PRINT B

    160 END

Transpose

The form of this matrix operation is

    MAT V = TRN(B)

The matrix B is transposed, and the result is assigned to the matrix V. The matrices V and B must be dimensioned. Those dimensions are the ones used.

Mat Input

The MAT INPUT statement permits the entry of values into a single-dimensioned array while the program is actually being executed. At the conclusion of the input, a variable NUM contains a number that tells the number of values that were entered. If the programmer wishes to enter no values, he simply returns the carriage. NUM will then contain the value zero. Here's an example:

```
100 DIM D(20)

110 MAT INPUT D

120 IF NUM = 0 THEN 180

130 LET J = NUM

140 FOR K = 1 TO J

150 PRINT D(K)

160 NEXT K

170 GO TO 110

180 END
```

CHAPTER 19

ALPHANUMERIC STATEMENTS

Up to this point, the values you've dealt with have all been *numeric.* It is possible to work with values that are *alphanumeric;* that is, values that are used not for computations, but for other purposes.

Consider this simple example:

```
10 LET A$ = "FOURSCORE AND"
20 LET B$ = "SEVEN"
30 LET C$ = "YEARS AGO"
40 PRINT A$;B$;C$
50 END
```

The program will print these words on the output paper:

```
FOURSCORE ANDSEVENYEARS AGO
```

As you can see, instead of assigning numeric values to memory cells, we assigned English words. The assigned words were enclosed in quotation marks. The names of the memory cells used included appended dollar signs ($). They were A$, B$, and C$.

If you intend to assign a word, catalog number, address, or some other alphanumeric message to a name, that name must have a dollar sign appended to it. Otherwise, the rules you used for creating variable names are still applicable. These names are correct for use with alphanumeric information:

> P$
> D3$
> L5$
> Q$

These are not:

D *(needs* a dollar sign)

DY$ (the D must be followed by a digit)

D3A$ (the name is too long)

The values you assign to a name may contain up to 60 characters (more on some systems). For example, this assignment is all right:

100 LET W$ = "THERE IS AN ERROR ON THE DATA LINE"

Whenever the user desires to print the above error message, he may give the command:

705 PRINT W$

Spaces given within quotation marks print in the corresponding positions of a print line. Consider, for example, how we may improve the program that was presented at the beginning of this chapter. The way the assignments were made to A$, B$, and C$ caused some words to run together. To make the output line more readable, we need blanks between the words AND and SEVEN, and SEVEN and YEARS. We may obtain these blanks by changing the assignment statements at line 10 and 20 to read as follows:

10 LET A$ = "FOURSCORE AND "

20 LET B$ = "SEVEN "

Observe the single blanks following the words AND and SEVEN. When we tell the computer to run this program, we will get this output:

```
FOURSCORE AND SEVEN YEARS AGO
```

There are other ways to make the change. For example, we could simply change line 20 to read:

    20 LET B$ = " SEVEN "

There are now blanks before and after the word SEVEN.

Alphanumeric values may be read from the DATA statement. Study this example:

    10 DATA THE INSTRUCTION, AT THE END OF

    20 DATA THE PROGRAM, SHOULD BE CHANGED

    30 DATA TO END

    40 READ A$, B$, C$, D$, E$

    50 PRINT A$; B$; C$; D$; E$

    60 END

The program assigns THE INSTRUCTION to A$, AT THE END OF to B$, THE PROGRAM to C$, SHOULD BE CHANGED to D$, and TO END to E$. Then it prints those values as follows:

```
THE INSTRUCTIONAT THE END OFTHE PROGRAMSHOULD BE CHANGEDTO END
```

You can see that we have some spacing problems because of the way the data values were read. Alternatively, we may place quotation marks around any data values in the DATA statement even though quotes may not strictly be needed. Let's change the DATA statement just a bit:

10 DATA "THE INSTRUCTION", " AT THE END OF"

20 DATA " THE PROGRAM", " SHOULD BE CHANGED"

30 DATA " TO END"

Blanks have been inserted before the A in AT, the T in THE, the S in SHOULD, and the T in TO. These blanks will appear on the output paper when we print A$ through E$. The output will look like this:

THE INSTRUCTION AT THE END OF THE PROGRAM SHOULD BE CHANGED TO END

Values in a DATA statement are separated by commas. If a data value is a pure numeric item or if it has characters that might cause confusion, the programmer must place quotes around the values. For example, consider these values, which we wish to assign to X$, Y$, and Z$:

10 DATA "3XLD" , "TROY, N.Y." , "74 FOX AVE"

Commas ordinarily separate data values, but the comma in Troy, N.Y. will not cause any confusion since the value is in quotes.

Once an alphanumeric value has been read, one may test it with IF statements like the following:

300 IF X$ = "JOHN WILLIAMS" THEN 600

310 IF Y$ = Z$ THEN 1600

320 IF Z$ > X$ THEN 2600

An alphanumeric value may be tested to determine whether it is equal to some other value. It may also be tested to determine whether it is smaller or larger than some other value. In BASIC, an alphanumeric value is greater than another alphanumeric value it if is higher in the *official collating scale*. This scale designates that digits are smaller than all letters of the alphabet. A digit or a letter is larger

144

than another if it is naturally higher up in the scale. Thus, 671 is greater than 421 and JONES is greater than BUTLER.

Let's try a problem. Suppose we have these data values in a DATA statement:

```
400 DATA ABE, JOHN, WILL, ANN, BETTY, TOM

410 DATA MARY, HELEN, SALLY, KEN, BEN, LUCY
```

These names identify students in a social science class. The class is working on four projects. Three students are assigned to each project. Thus, students ABE, JOHN, and WILL are on the first project; ANN, BETTY, and TOM are on the second project, etc.

We need a program that identifies the other two students on a project when the name of one student is input from the keyboard.

Example:

If the name SALLY is input, the program gives student names MARY, HELEN, and SALLY. The program must also tell which project is involved.   The flowchart for this program is on the next page.

Here is the program:

```
400 DATA ABE, JOHN, WILL, ANN, BETTY, TOM
410 DATA MARY, HELEN, SALLY, KEN, BEN, LUCY
420 INPUT X$
430 IF X$ = "END" THEN 550
440 FOR C = 1 TO 4
450 READ A$, B$, C$
460 IF X$ = A$ THEN 530
470 IF X$ = B$ THEN 530
480 IF X$ = C$ THEN 530
490 NEXT C
500 PRINT "NAME NOT IN DATA", X$
510 RESTORE$
520 GO TO 420
530 PRINT A$, B$, C$, C
540 GO TO 510
550 END
```

145

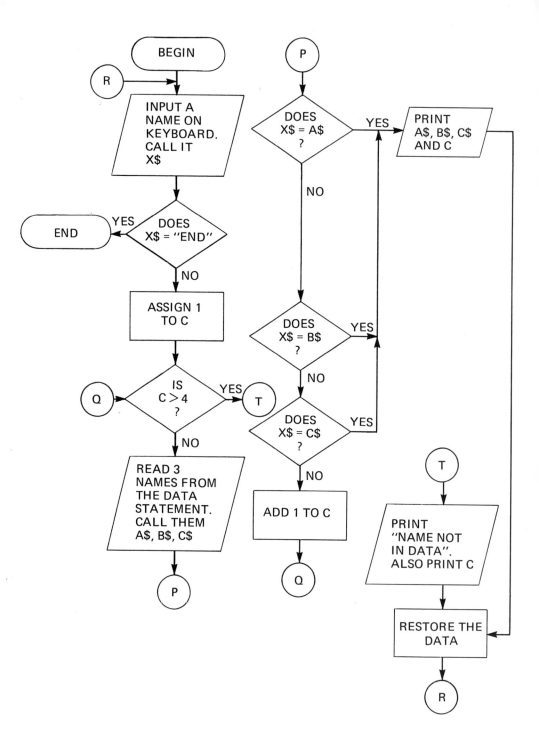

The RESTORE\$ statement at line 150 restores alphanumeric data in a program just as RESTORE restores numeric data. RESTORE and

RESTORE$ act independently of each other. A DATA statement may contain both numeric and alphanumeric values. The names to which those values are assigned must match the values.

Example:

10 DATA THE, BEST, 3345, JOBS, ARE, "3345", HERE

may be read with this READ statement:

20 READ E$, F$, X, G$, H$, K$, L$

The value X may be used in calculations, but K$ may not. (X is a pure numeric value, while K$ is alphanumeric.)

Alphanumeric arrays may be established should they be required.

Example:

```
 10 DATA MARY, ALLEN, ROBERT, INGALLS, OLIVER, XAVIER
 20 DATA FRED, ANDERSON, RICHARD, ILLY, NELSON, AMES
 30 DATA LUCY, MAPES, NED, CONNERS, PETE, MILLS
 40 DATA FRED, TIMS
 50 DIM F$(10), L$(10)
 60 FOR N = 1 TO 10
 70 READ F$(N), L$(N)
 80 NEXT N
 90 INPUT X$
100 IF X$ = "DONE" THEN 180
110 FOR K = 1 TO 10
120 IF X$ = F$(K) THEN 160
130 NEXT K
140 PRINT "NAME NOT FOUND", X$
150 GO TO 90
160 PRINT X$, F$(K),L$(K)
170 GO TO 90
180 END
```

This program gives a person's last name when the first name is entered via the terminal's keyboard.

CHAPTER 20

THE *GOSUB, RETURN,* AND *ON* STATEMENTS

The GOSUB statement is very much like a simple GO TO statement. The single difference is that in the former, when the program is instructed to go to the new point in the program, the program records the point from where the jump was made. It later returns automatically to that point. Go to statements, on the other hand, cause a program to continue processing from the point where the jump was made.

Here is a skeleton outline of a program showing how GOSUB works:

```
10  ~~~~~~~
20  ~~~~~~~
30  ~~~~~~~
40  GOSUB  2000
50  ~~~~~~~
60  ~~~~~~~
70  ~~~~~~~
80  GOSUB 2000
90  ~~~~~~~
100 ~~~~~~~
110 ~~~~~~~
120 ~~~~~~~
```

```
130  GOSUB 2000
140  〜〜〜〜
150  〜〜〜〜
160  GO TO 3000
2000 〜〜〜〜
2010 〜〜〜〜
2020 〜〜〜〜
2030 〜〜〜〜
2040 RETURN
3000 END
```

The wavy lines indicate statements which are not germane to this discussion and are therefore not shown in detail.

The program begins at line 10 and executes BASIC statements until it reaches line 40. The program then jumps to line 2000 (GOSUB 2000). The program executes the statements beginning with 2000 and encounters the RETURN statement at line 2040. This statement causes the program to go back to line 50. Observe that line 50 is the line immediately following line 40, the line that contains the GOSUB statement.

Beginning at line 50, the program now advances to line 80 where it finds another GOSUB statement, GOSUB 2000. The program again jumps to line 2000 and progresses from that point to line 2040. The RETURN statement found there causes the program to jump to line 90, the statement immediately following the second GOSUB statement.

From 90, the program now advances to line 130 where a third GOSUB is found. The program again jumps to line 2000, and when the RETURN statement is encountered for the third time, the program returns to line 140.

Finally, the program executes all the statements between 140 and 160. The GO TO statement at line 160 instructs the computer to jump directly to the END statement at line 3000. It is important that a GO TO statement appear before statement 2000; otherwise, the program would once more go into the group of statements beginning at line 2000. This time, the RETURN statement at line 2040 would cause trouble because the RETURN statement there cannot be matched against any GOSUB previously given.

The GOSUB statement may be used to instruct the computer to go to a group of statements known as a *subroutine*. Subroutines are used to provide a group of instructions that may be accessed from various parts of the program. Let's study an example: Suppose we have this DATA statement:

    100 DATA 18,1,14,2,7,3,4,17,2,8,2

    110 DATA 10,3,7,32,1,14,3,8,9999,0

Our program is to read two data values using the following READ statement:

    120 READ X,C

X is a numeric value, while C is a code that instructs what must be done with the value. If the value of C is 1, X is to act as the radius of a circle, and the program must compute the area of the circle:

$$A = 3.1416 * X \uparrow 2$$

If the value of C is 2, X is to act as the length of one side of a square, and the program must compute the area of the square:

$$A = X * X$$

If the value of C is 3, X is to act as the length of one side of a right triangle. The program is to obtain the next value in the DATA statement, then compute the area of the triangle:

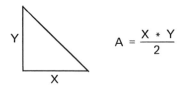

$$A = \frac{X * Y}{2}$$

We may use this flowchart:

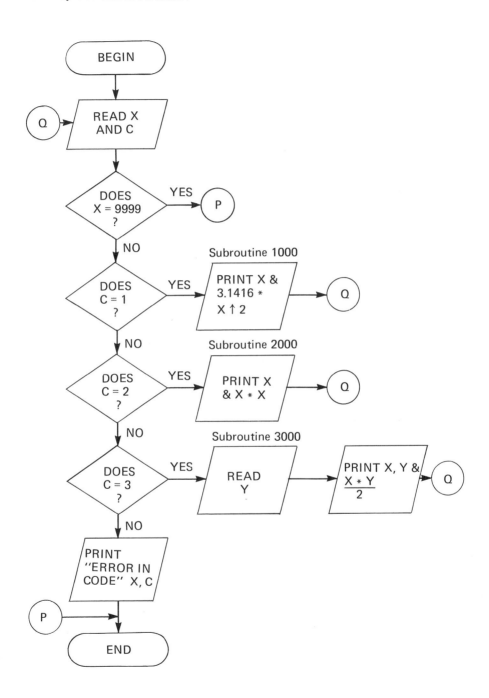

The corresponding program is:

153

```
100  DATA 18,1,14,2,7,3,4,17,2,8,2
110  DATA 10,3,7,32,1,14,3,8,9999,0
120  READ X,C
130  IF X = 9999 THEN 4000
140  IF C = 1 THEN 200
150  IF C = 2 THEN 300
160  IF C = 3 THEN 400
170  PRINT "ERROR IN CODE",X,C
180  GO TO 4000
200  GOSUB 1000
210  GO TO 120
300  GOSUB 2000
310  GO TO 120
400  GOSUB 3000
410  GO TO 120
1000 PRINT X, 3.1416*X↑2
1010 RETURN
2000 PRINT X, X*X
2010 RETURN
3000 READ Y
3010 PRINT X, Y, (X*Y)/2
3020 RETURN
4000 END
```

The program will give this output:

18	1017.88			
14	196			
7	4	14		
17	289			
8	64			
10	7	35		
32	3217			
14	8	56		

154

We could have written this program more simply without using subroutines. Though this problem solution did not actually require subroutines, we wrote it this way simply to demonstrate how subroutines function.

Subroutines may call other subroutines. The RETURN statement always sends the program back to the statement immediately following the GOSUB that called the subroutine. There may be any number of subroutines in a program accessed by GOSUBs.

Another way to write the example program given above is by using the ON statement. Here is the program:

```
100  DATA 18,1,14,2,7,3,4,17,2,8,2

110  DATA 10,3,7,32,1,14,3,8,9999,0

120  READ X,C

130  ON C GO TO 1000, 2000, 3000

140  PRINT "ERROR IN CODE",X,C

150  GO TO 4000

1000  PRINT X,3.1416*X↑2

1010  GO TO 120

2000 PRINT X, X*X

2010  GO TO 120

3000  READ Y

3010  PRINT X,Y,(X*Y)/2

3020  GO TO 120

4000  END
```

The ON statement expects the name that follows the word ON to have the integer value 1, 2, 3, etc. If the value assigned to the name is 1, the program will jump to the first line number shown after the words GO TO; if the value is 2, to the second line number, etc.

There may be several line numbers following the words GO TO, but as many as there are, the value of the code must have a way to reach them all. For example, if we have

50 ON K GO TO 100, 150, 200, 250, 300

the value of K must at one time or another be equal to the integer value 1, 2, 3, 4, or 5. The value of the code must be neither negative nor a value larger than the number of line numbers following GO TO. If these illegal conditions are present, the program does not jump to a distant area of the program; instead, it goes to the next statement in sequence.

If the code following ON is a mixed number (for example, 3.6), the program *truncates* (chops off) the fractional part of the code and uses the value that's left. Thus, in our example, when the code is 3.6, the fractional part of the code is chopped off and the 3 that remains acts as the final code that is actually used.

CHAPTER 21

WORKING WITH PAPER TAPE

Many terminals provide the facility to punch programs on paper tape. The kind of paper tape one may obtain and the actual procedure for obtaining it vary from terminal to terminal. This chapter will concern itself only with obtaining paper tape from the Model 33 Teletype.

This is the type of paper tape we are discussing:

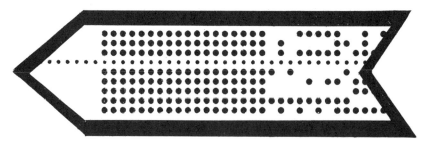

Punched paper tape may be used to:

1. Save programs.
2. Enter programs into the system instead of manually typing the information while *on-line.*

Suppose you wish to save on paper tape a program that you have created and saved in the system. The procedure is this:

1. Turn ON the paper tape punch unit.

2. Simultaneously depress the four keys CTRL, SHIFT, RPT, and P. Hold down the keys until you obtain about 20 or 30 characters. You'll note that this procedure gives you some blank tape that you may use to hand-print the name of the program, date, etc.

3. Simultaneously depress the two keys RUBOUT and RPT and hold them down until you've obtained about 20 RUBOUT characters on the paper tape.

4. Turn the punch unit OFF.

5. Depress the RETURN key.

6. Now, type LIST and then return the carriage. A fraction of a second later turn the paper tape punch unit ON.

7. Wait until the system has completely punched your program on paper tape.

8. Next, give about 20 more RUBOUT characters.

9. Then, turn the punch unit OFF. Return the carriage. Tear off the paper tape. Label the tape and save it for a future application.

Suppose you must create a paper tape off-line. Follow these steps:

1. Set the mode switch of the teletype on LOCAL.

2. Depress the four keys CTRL, SHIFT, RPT, and P as you did before and hold them down until you obtain about 20 or 30 characters. You have received a blank area at the beginning of your tape for hand-labelling.

3. Depress the RPT and RUBOUT keys and hold them down until about 20 RUBOUT characters have been punched.

4. Return the carriage.

5. Type a line of your program.

6. Give a line feed using the LINE FEED key.

7. Return the carriage again.

8. Give an XOFF character (by depressing the keys CTRL and S simultaneously).

9. Give one RUBOUT character.

10. Repeat steps 5 through 9 as often as necessary to build your program.

11. At the conclusion of the tape, call for 20 or so additional RUBOUTs.

12. Tear off the tape, label it, and then turn the teletype OFF.

Character-delete control characters (←) may be given in the usual way. Line-delete controls, though, must be used as follows:

1. Type the line (to be deleted).
2. Give line-delete control (by depressing the keys CTRL and X).
3. Give an XOFF character (by depressing CTRL and S).
4. Give a RUBOUT character.
5. Type the corrected line.
6. Give a line feed by depressing the LINE FEED key.
7. Give a carriage return.
8. Give another XOFF character.
9. Give one RUBOUT character.

To read a paper tape into the timesharing system, follow these steps:

1. Position the paper tape on the paper tape reader so that the read head lies directly over RUBOUT characters.
2. Place the reader switch on the paper tape reader on the FREE position.
3. Type NEW. The system will respond READY.
4. Type the word TAPE.
5. When the system types READY, flip the reader switch to START. The entire tape will read in.
6. Return the carriage.

There may be difficulties. At those times, the user should take various kinds of actions depending upon what the problem is. If the system seems to "die" after a tape has been read, type an XOFF character (by depressing CTRL and S). If the system doesn't respond, try to get its attention by giving a carriage return or a BREAK.

Dealing with paper tape is a little tricky; but after you've created a few tapes and read them into the system, you'll probably have no further difficulty.

Once paper tape has been mastered, its use will save you money. For input to timesharing, a tape punched off-line is cheaper to read in because the system reads the paper tape faster than you can type. For output, programs saved on tape cost nothing, whereas programs saved in the system cost at least $2.00 per month per program. If you run a program infrequently, saving it on paper tape is definitely cheaper; you read it in only when you need it.

CHAPTER 22

DEFINED FUNCTIONS

In previous chapters, we discussed several functions built into the BASIC language. These were SIN, COS, SQR, etc. Here, for convenience, is a complete list of the *built-in functions* along with a brief summary of what they may be used for. (The information supplied within parentheses for each of these functions is called the *argument of the function.*)

Function	*Purpose*
SIN (X)	Compute the sine of X. X may be an actual number or BASIC name or expression. X must be given in radian measure.
COS (X)	Compute the cosine of X. X may be a value as described under SIN (X).
TAN (X)	Compute the tangent of X. X may be a value as described under SIN (X)
ATN (X)	Compute the arctangent of X. X may be an actual number or a BASIC name or an expression. The arctangent of X is given in radian measure.
EXP (X)	Compute e^X. The value of X may be an actual number or a BASIC name or an expression. The value of e is 2.718281828 . . . .
ABS (X)	Obtain the absolute value of X. X may be a value as described under EXP (X).

Function	Purpose
LOG (X)	Compute the natural log of X. X may be a value as described under EXP (X).
SQR (X)	Compute the square root of X. X may be a value as described under EXP (X).
RND (X)	Obtain a random number. The number lies between zero and one. It may be zero, but it may never actually be one. Type RANDOM on the first line of your program if you want non-repeatable numbers.
INT (X)	Obtain the largest integer from X. X may be a value as described under EXP (X).

If a function you would like to use in a program is not available in the list of functions given above, you may define your own function. Near the beginning of your program you may write a statement similar to this one:

```
100 DEF FNA (L) = (SIN(L) + COS (L))/4
```

You have invented a function named FNA. This function may now be used anywhere in your program that you need to add the sine and cosine of a value and divide the result by 4.

The reason this function doesn't already exist in BASIC is that among programmers there's little need for such a function. Nevertheless, *you* may need this function many times for a special program you are working on. If so, BASIC enables you to invent a function to use for the duration of the one program only. If you should need the very same function in another program, you would have to define it all over again in that new program.

Having defined a function, you are now interested in how to use it. Use a defined function the same way that you use a built-in function; that is, if you have functions defined as FNB, FND, and FNQ, you may use them in the following ways:

```
200 LET F = FNB(2.5) + SIN(D)

210 LET H = FND(L+M)

220 LET K = FNQ(N) − SQR(P)
```

The values placed within parentheses of defined functions may be actual numeric values or BASIC names or expressions. These values constitute the arguments of the defined functions.

As you can see, functions must be defined near the beginning of a program—or at least before the function is actually used in the program. When you name a function, the name you give it must begin with FN. The third and final character in the name may be any letter of the alphabet.

In the definition of the function, the single letter placed within parentheses is a dummy character. It has no purpose other than to show how actual values, when given, will be manipulated. Thus, the definition for FNA given above was

```
100 DEF FNA(L) = (SIN(L)+COS(L))/4
```

L is not an actual value. It is a *placeholder,* showing that when another value such as (P–Q)/R is given for use in the function, such as:

```
350 LET G = FNA((P–Q)/R)
```

the value of (P–Q)/R will first be computed; then the sin and cosine of the value will be obtained. Those values will be summed, and the result divided by 4. In short, L stands for (P–Q)/R in this instance. Later in the program, if the statement

```
850 LET Z = FNA(S)
```

were executed, the value of S would be handled the same way as L is handled in the definition of a function; that is, the value Z would be computed from

```
(SIN(S)+COS(S))/4
```

As in SQR, SIN, COS, and all the other built-in functions, only one value may be used in both the definition of a function and its use.

CHAPTER 23

FILE HANDLING STATEMENTS

There are six statement types that permit dealing with files. These are FILES, READ, WRITE, SCRATCH, RESTORE, and IF.

But first we have to understand what a file is. A *file* is a series of saved lines that contain numbers. These numbers are saved under some name in the same way that programs are saved.

Suppose we wish to save this file:

Employee Number	Pay Rate
265	3.15
300	4.05
315	2.95
335	3.80
450	5.50
480	4.30
515	3.75
575	4.15

We could type it in the same way that we would type a program:

```
100  265,  3.15,
200  300,  4.05,
300  315,  2.95,
```

167

```
400  335,  3.80,
500  450,  5.50,
600  480,  4.30,
700  515,  3.75,
800  575,  4.15,
```

The numbers 100, 200, etc., are line numbers—files require line numbers just as programs do. On each line of the file, the first number following the line number represents the employee number and the next number represents the pay rate. Observe that commas follow all data values, but they do not follow line numbers.

Now we may save the file by typing SAVE. Any name we select as the name of a file is all right. That name may have up to six characters consisting of letters of the alphabet and digits. Assume that we named this file MASTER.

Now we may type another file containing this information:

Employee Number	Hours Worked
265	38.5
300	41.5
315	40.0
335	39.0
450	40.5
480	40.0
515	42.5
575	37.5

The file may be typed and saved in the same way that MASTER was saved. We may type:

```
100  265,  38.5,
200  300,  41.5,
300  315,  40.0,
400  335,  39.0,
500  450,  40.5,
600  480,  40.0,
700  515,  42.5,
800  575,  37.5,
```

Assume that we named this file TRANS.

Now we may type a program that reads a line from file MASTER and a line from file TRANS and computes gross pay. Then we will record the information in a new file called NEWFIL.

We'll give the program and then explain it:

```
100 FILES MASTER;TRANS;NEWFIL
110 SCRATCH #3
120 IF END #1 THEN 210
130 READ #1, E1, R
140 READ #2, E2, H
150 IF E1 < > E2 THEN 200
160 LET G = H*R
170 WRITE #3, E1, H, R, G
180 PRINT E1, H, R, G
190 GO TO 120
200 PRINT "ERROR IN FILE.  EMPLOYEE NUMS DISAGREE."
210 END
```

The FILES statement at line 100 gives the names of the files that will be used in the lines that follow. It must be the very first statement of the program. Observe that the names of the files are separated by semicolons.

In the program, when #1 is referenced (see line 130), the file referred to is the first one in the FILES statement, MASTER; whenever #2 is referenced (see line 140), the file referred to is the second one in the FILES statement, TRANS; and, whenever #3 is referenced (see line 170), the file referred to is NEWFIL.

It is important to understand that files always exist in one of two modes—*read* and *write*. A file in read mode may be read, but not written upon; a file in write mode may be written upon, but not read. Initially, all files are in read mode. Therefore, in order that a file might be written upon, it must be changed from read mode to write mode. The SCRATCH statement at line 110 accomplishes this task for file #3 (NEWFIL). If a file is not changed from read mode to write mode, the program will not write upon it. An error message will be given when such an attempt is made.

The SCRATCH command may be given anywhere in a program—so long as it is given ahead of the program's attempt to write upon the file.

If a file is in write mode and one desires to change the file to read mode, the programmer gives the RESTORE command:

RESTORE #3

Keep in mind that initially all files are in read mode and the RESTORE command is not needed before the corresponding files are read.

The IF END statement checks a file to determine whether there is more information upon it that may be read. The form of the statement is

IF END #1 THEN 800

If the statement detects that the end of the file has been reached (that is, that there is no more data in the file to be read), the program jumps to line 800; otherwise, the program goes on to the next statement in sequence.

In the example program, the IF END statement is at line 120. The statement checks file #1, MASTER, to determine whether the applicable READ statement at line 130 should be executed. The program goes on to the next statement in sequence if the end of file #1 has not been found; it goes to statement 210 if the end of file #1 has been found.

The check for "end of file" is placed *ahead* of the applicable READ statement. An error message will be given if an attempt is made to read a file that has no data left in it to be read.

The WRITE statement at line 170 causes the entry of a line of output in the file referenced, NEWFIL. The output line will have a line number (the system gives line 10 as the first line number, and line numbers increase by 10 units) followed by the values named. In the example, those values are E1, H, R, and G.

This program also prints the same line that has been recorded in the file. The PRINT statement is optional. A program may write into a file but not print the same line, or it may simply print a line without writing it into a file, or it may do both.

Now about the program itself. The program reads a line from

170

MASTER and a line from TRANS. It then has the following information in its memory:

From MASTER	E1 = 265
	R = 3.15
From TRANS	E2 = 265
	H = 38.5

The value 265 represents the employee number found on the first line of each file. This program requires that the two numbers agree. If they don't, the program assumes that a serious discrepancy exists, and the program stops. If the numbers do agree, then 3.15 found in the master file represents the pay rate per hour of employee 265, and 38.5 represents hours worked last week by the same employee. The program computes gross pay, G, for employee 265. Then it writes four values into NEWFIL: employee number, hours worked, pay rate, and gross pay. The program also prints a line on the output paper, giving the same information.

The program returns to the IF END statement to repeat the cycle if more data exists in file #1. When the data is exhausted in file #1, the program jumps to the END statement, and the job is terminated.

To determine whether the program has created NEWFIL properly, one may call for NEWFIL this way:

OLD NEWFIL

and then have the system list it. The programmer types

LIST

NEWFIL contains up-to-date information concerning the employees whose records were found in the MASTER and TRANS files. NEWFIL may therefore be used as the input data to some other program that the user might want to write.

File-handling commands differ slightly from system to system. If the commands shown in this chapter don't work on your system, contact your representative, your instructor, or a fellow user. You'll find that the differences are slight and easy to master.

INDEX

173

174